Maura,

IT was a great Experience
working with you. Cheers for
all your Enthusiasm, Energy and
work. Enjoy the week es
Valarie but leave it in the
theatre and Enjoy the fun!

TURBULENCE

TURBULENCE

CORRIB VOICES
edited by Helena Mulkerns

Siar Press

First published by Siar Press 2003

Siar Press
Menlough, Ballinasloe
Co. Galway, Ireland
http://siar.net/turbulence.htm

Edited by Helena Mulkerns
Design, cover and photographs by Helena Mulkerns
All cover photos feature the waters of the Corrib River, Galway

ISBN 0-9545620-0-3

Printed by Publish on Demand Ltd.
http://publish-on-demand.co.uk

DEDICATED TO THE MEMORY OF

Jim Mulkerns
1927-2003

THANK YOU

Kevin Barry, Ramon Bonet, Dermot Bolger, Catherine Byrne,
Susanne Carbin, Julia Carlson, Erin Carstens, Angela Carter,
Ciaran Carty, Stephen Cary, Lucrezia Conklin,
Roger Derham, Anne Ennis, Aoife Faherty, Adrian Frazier,
Aidan Hynes, Derval Kennedy, Melissa Knight,
Katherine Laing, Scott Malcolm, Colum McCann,
Mike McCormack, John Montague, Dearbhla Mooney,
Doug Mulkerns, Helen Mulkerns, Val Mulkerns,
Deirdre Nolan, Gordon Snell, Jennifer Smith, Eddie Stack,
Robert Symth, Mike Tobin, Elizabeth Tilley, Jonathan Williams,

and all the contributers

TABLE OF CONTENTS

TABLE OF CONTENTS continued

INTRODUCTION

Mike McCormack

Anthologies of new writing are some of the more delicate, lovingly nurtured blooms on the cultural landscape. They prove that out there, valiant believers give of their time and a type hectoring patience to bring voices out of lonely rooms. Like pirate radio stations which giddy the ether from time to time with their contrary voices and rhythms, they function as a kind of samizdat within the open consensus of this province. Tuning into them makes you complicit in a healthy underground. It marks you out as curious, unsatisfied with the current wisdom, anxious to hear voices in utero, avid to catch imaginations on the wing. The importance of such anthologies to writers, established and beginner, is beyond measure. They provide a type of proving ground where new work can be exposed to an audience who know full well that this same work has not received its final polish. Thus there is a type of critical latitude between the writer and his audience — they enter into a tentative partnership with each other. One is anxious for feedback, while the other hankers after new voices and ideas. Both hope for new perspectives.

Turbulence is a classy addition to this tradition. It brings poetry, fiction and prose reflections by seasoned and first time writers, together within the curve of the biggest waterway in the province. It is a welcome addition to the cultural landscape of the west. It carefully showcases the work within a vigilant editorial matrix which ensures that it is a book any writer would be proud to have their work included in. Some writers are publishing their first work in this anthology — it is a heady start, a major step up from small magazines or newspaper competitions. There are few thrills to equal seeing your first published poem or short story and a publication this cool and considered can be marked up as a something of a flying start.

In keeping with its brave origins the anthology delivers a variety of voices. Too often in the minds of readers and writers, anthologists and editors, these traditions have been artificially segregated as if they had nothing to say to each other or, worse, learn from each other. *Turbulence* cuts through these snobberies, refusing to recognise the ghetto mentality that tends to thwart dialogue. And while no one wants poetic prose or prosaic poetry — those etiolated hybrids — it is surely the case that in matters of theme and sensibility some type of fruitful intercourse can be hoped for. The alternate positioning of the pieces in this collection is the kind of forced intimacy which may lead to a fruitful cross fertilisation.

As you might expect, there is a diversity of concern and topography. Themes of love and loss sit cheek by jowl with tales of feminine retribution and obsession. Middle age men cosy up to cool chicks. The West of Ireland broadens out into the wider spaces of the Canadian wilderness. This is of a piece with the wide demographic covered in the anthology. The mood is twitchy, imaginatively engaged but far flung. There is no binding theme, no running concern, no attempt to marshal individual voices into an artificially binding theme. This is as it should be. Anthologies of this type thrive on dissonance and jostling antipathies. Ideas bounce off each other, they gain light and shade from their neighbours, hopefully they will revisit each other in the future at some time known only to themselves.

It comes with a fitting title — the rise and fall of its differing genres mirroring the contending moods of the Corrib itself. Colours and rhythms displace each other in a warp and weft known only to itself. It is a book to be dipped into and savoured in quiet moments, a book for passing around in coffee houses and gatherings, and it will stand as a valuable record of these writers at a particular stage of their development. Read and enjoy.

GETTING LOST IN CADIZ

Misja Weesjes

It is said that when the sun sets in Cádiz, it falls off the edge of the world. How it manages to climb back up again each morning no one knows, but the fall is always a magnificent sight. That is, if you happen to be within sight of the sea.

You could be sitting outside the little fisherman's bar on the Playa de la Caleta, for example, with a cold beer on the table beside you, and little fishing boats bobbing in the sea in front of the fort of San Sebastián, behind which the orange sun falls. Better still, you could take a stroll along the miles of beaches that run along the southern edge of the city. Here every evening, the locals go on their daily *paseo*, immaculately groomed, with beautifully dressed children and pedigreed dogs.

Stray more than a few paces from the city's edge, however, and you lose sight of both sea and sun, and are immediately swallowed up into the warren of narrow, cobbled, one-way streets that is the old part of Cádiz. As you walk along these little streets, dodging twenty year-old cars and innumerable scooters adorned with handsome young Spaniards, your eye will constantly be drawn to the old and dilapidated, yet still somehow beautiful buildings that make up the ancient port. Elaborately carved doorways support massive oak doors, behind which, more often than not, are little hidden courtyards embellished with Andalusian tile work and earthenware pots, overflowing with flowers and greenery.

If you happen to look up, you will see a thin strip of blue sky, on either side of which drape down these buildings, hiding ornately rusted balconies behind weathered wooden blinds. The

song of caged birds floats down and adds a sort of timelessness to your impressions as you walk.

Cádiz is not a town that moves with the times. Its inhabitants do — slowly, years behind everyone else — but the town itself does not shake off its past.

When, unexpectedly (for you think you know where you are going), you come upon one of the many scattered plazas — little and not so little, but never big — the slight sense of claustrophobia experienced in the streets fades, but you will still not be able to get your bearing from the sun. The plazas are not big enough for it ever to be visible among the tall, tall palm trees and oaks which adorn them.

You sit down at a little table and order a nice cold *caña*, which inevitably comes with a little plate of olives, take out your map, and get your bearings. Then, when you've drunk your fill and found on the map both where you are and where you want to go, you confidently set off.

Five minutes later you are lost again.

Getting lost in Cádiz, however, is a rather pleasant experience. The town, surrounded almost entirely by water, has expanded only outside the old city walls along the narrow strip of land that joins it to the mainland, and you can, in theory, walk from one end to the other in fifteen minutes. Unless you unknowingly come within yards of the sea and your bearings, that is, and take a wrong turn, which takes you back into the heart of the town.

You don't mind too much though, for you will inevitably find the little church which was impossible to find on your last walk, and which provides some stunning examples of Catholic ornamentation at its baroque best. Or you might happen upon the Plaza de las Flores, which stubbornly resists being called by its newer name, Plaza de la Topete, and that is still covered with flower stalls. Then, unexpectedly, you will find yourself on the promenade — albeit the one on a different side of the town than you thought you were heading for — and you will know that if you walk along the beach, in just a few minutes you will again be within sight of the playa you meant to go to, where you can sit on the beach, a cold beer in your hand, and watch the sun fall off again.

THERE ARE NO SEAGULLS IN TOTNES TODAY

Dawn breaks in a misty silence.
people rise into routine
vaguely aware that something is missing.

Nothing perches on roof tops and
telegraph poles
looking down on the town.

And there are fewer greetings
and more
glances.

As an old woman makes her hunched way
up the steep high street
past the abandoned church.

And the day drifts by
as wind
through a chimney.

The sun falls, and Totnes gets an early night,
where lovers lay without touching.
in the silence.

SHADOW

I am not your lover
You are not mine
Given enough shadow
Given enough time.

BARRY FERNS

ODE TO MARLBORO LIGHTS

It seems to me so long ago
That I held you close, so tight
And I've been so desperate
Since that stormy Tuesday night

I miss your touch, I miss your smell
I miss the taste you leave behind
I really miss your warmth as well
Hanging loose beneath my eyes

In a dream I find in vain
All the nights we spent together
The long thin wafer body that leaves
Your smell upon my sweater

But most of all I miss
Setting fire to your head
And sucking the life out of you.

OWNING THE LOCUS

Cool in the pounding desert heat
in your skeleton leaf dress.
Cool when the empty sky brings frost.
The night is moonless.
You are just enough light
for me to see by.

BARRY FERNS

16

THE MEN IN MY LIFE

Susan Lanigan

There have been many lovers through the years whom I remember with affection, but if you were to ask me which one made the difference in my life, I'd have to say John Scales. Funny, because he definitely is not my grand passion. Just the one who hung around longest, when all is said and done.

He's got no great imagination when it comes to the more intimate parts of life. Straight up and down has always been his motto. In and out he goes, in a regimental fashion, always the same way, always the same strokes. It gets so boring. There have been times I have found myself well able to concentrate on something else entirely while he was at it. I worked out a whole new design for my kitchen once while he was banging away with his usual rhythmical fervour. When I get myself a cup of coffee and admire the cheery yellow colour scheme, I remember him with affection.

He is the only English one. I'm English too and it binds us together in a way, because there are things I don't have to explain to him. He gets the whole irony thing in a way the others never could — he even laughs at the way I play him so well. The others were all foreigners. Englishmen don't do it for me, for some reason, but even with that I still like to see old John from time to time.

I popped my cherry to a German guy called Wolf. Well, a few minutes after being in a clinch with the guy, I just fell about laughing. Wolf, indeed! He was enthusiastic, but lacked the savagery one would expect from a name like that. I proposed renaming him Tabby Cat and he took it in good humour. Always a challenge, he was, a bit impossibly light-hearted but intelligent all the same. "I'm an Aquarius, dear," he told me, as an explanation. "We're people of the air." I'm a Scorpio, myself, so I like it down and dirty; he would have been way too fastidious to try anything like that.

That said, Wolf did do the dirt on me in the end. There was my pretty friend Svetlana from Bulgaria, impossibly supple with hands that looked as if they would stroke you into a state of blissful unconsciousness. He flashed me barely a grin of apology and off he went. She understood him better, apparently. But by then I didn't mind because I'd met Lou, who turned out to be the first big love of my life.

Lou was talented, passionate and so totally messed up I couldn't help falling for him like a ton of bricks. He could make anything come to life. I remember the morning after a night's crazy passion — God we tried *everything* — when a little yellowhammer sat on the tree outside my window and started chirrupping something. Lou sat bolt upright on the messy bed and listened. "Tee-tee-tee *too*" the bird trilled and I could see his eyes light up as he grasped my arm. "That's *music*, Natasha!" I remember him saying.

He used to murmur to me in a terrible (but terribly sexy) Italian accent *si deve suonare tutto questo pezzo delicatissimamente e senza sordini*. I hadn't a clue what he meant, but tried to come up with the goods. It was worth it just to hear him cry with joy. I thought nothing could be better than this. Even the worst bits were better than anything I'd ever known.

But it didn't last. Paradise never does, does it? Lou used to work days on a building site and one day he fell and suffered bad head injuries. He survived but suffered from blackouts and seizures. The worst bit was that he couldn't hear properly any more. It tore me apart, watching him rocking back and forth, head in his hands, crying out to make it stop.

Things changed between us too. Lou became increasingly distrusting and aggressive, shouting at me if I so much as dared to say hello to another guy in the street. Oh God, I'll never forget the day I brought Wolf over to cheer him up, thinking they'd combine well. That was a mistake. Wolf's nice little mannerisms turned into nervous tics under Lou's basilisk glare and after he slunk away, Lou hit me and I saw stars. That was the night I went away, telling Lou not to follow me. He didn't. I found out later that he died alone in his flat, just before he was due a doctor's appointment. Poor Lou. I know it's a cliché but he was too good, too sweet for this world — I still feel pain when I see the notes he scribbled down. I'll always keep them.

After Lou I had a bit of a nervous breakdown. There was nobody for a long time. Then, gradually, I answered the door when John came around to call. He'd been there through the whole mess with Lou and offered me a sensible shoulder to cry on whenever things got unbearable. "John," I used to joke with him, "you're not a real lover, you're more like my practice man between lovers." John, being an easygoing sort of person, took no offence at that comment. He offered me a lot of comfort, which was just what I needed. With his encouragement I moved to a bigger city and joined a musical society. And that's where I met Freddie.

The first reason I was attracted to him was his gentleness. After the storms and extremes of being with Lou, Freddie was like a pleasant summer evening. That's not to say he wasn't deep emotionally. He'd lived in France for a long time and was as romantic as any Frenchman even though he actually came from Eastern Europe. And he was gorgeous — he had a firm chin, aquiline nose and eyes that looked at you like liquid. When he and I were together in the heat of love, he would search me up and down and clasp me so passionately I could hardly breathe. His understanding of what a woman wanted was so accurate it took my breath away — every time.

The problem was that Freddie eventually changed from being intense to being intensely demanding. He was chasing this ideal woman in his head and would constantly test me to see if I were good enough. I could feel those wondrous eyes swivel to the floor with disappointment whenever I muffed up anything. I began to get nervous — dropping things, making noise, just clashing with the scenery, really. The writing was on the wall and I had to leave before I turned into a complete nervous wreck. Freddie, who had been waiting for me to get the hint, was relieved. We're friends now and still meet up from time to time. The truth, Freddie admitted to me once, is that he's never managed to hold down a relationship because he's never satisfied with what he has. He's like the knight in the tarot cards looking for another damsel in distress. He's managed to clock up a fair few as well since then, from what I hear.

So once again it was up to John to fill up the gap. This happened quite seamlessly; Freddie had always liked John and they often had a laugh together. I often suspected he liked John more than he liked me, but John's never let on and I don't ask. It was just John for a long time, though there was the odd dalliance with foreigners, like that French nutter Erik or Aaron. Aahh, Aaron ... the only American I ever got involved with. It didn't last long. I've nothing against Americans, but Aaron was so square. I think it was after he took me to a hoedown that I finished it. How could any man presume to understand me and take me line dancing? I don't see him at all any more, though I certainly wish him well, wherever he is now.

And so there they are, all of them. The men who moulded me, influenced me, changed me irrevocably. God bless them all, because without them I wouldn't be here today. I would not be sitting in this hall, at this piano, the orchestra assembled, the conductor ready to raise his baton. Nobody would have heard of Natasha Cantor, a name which, I can say with all modesty, is quite well known now.

They caused it all. The three great loves of my life: Wolfgang Amadeus Mozart, Ludwig van Beethoven, Frederic Chopin. Though they drove me crazy, I loved them with my heart and soul. I think I always will.

But in the end there's one person who got me here. And for all his up and down rhythm; endless battering, relentless technique; wittering on in thirds and in contrary motion and even in the occasional subtle chromatic — for all that he sometimes drove me up the wall, I would be *nothing* without boring, predictable old John Scales.

EQUUS

They said, he found it
not far from the estate —
a horse's head
shorn of all flesh
eyeless
in a slightly
imperfect socket —
and that he foolishly
tried it for size.

Then he grew
long-jawed
and ate apples whole
crunched raw carrots
to their green coronets.

Some said,
it was a mule's head
for he was
a truculent hybrid
and would do only
as he pleased.

He talked of politics
caustically
over the heads
of women
bent in worship
at their rosebeds
and crocuses in spring.

Some said,
he could canter:
others, that he shook
his head
and blew loudly
through his nose,
when aroused.

After a while
women observed,
though his jaw had slackened
that he kept retreating
and returning
in the heat of his chat.

He affected a walking stick
with a ferrule
in the shape
of a horse's hoof
he would not be happy
'til he got another
and could go on all fours
to the shop
for brown bread and cheese
and cut them like doorsteps.

He would eat them
with brown relish
awkwardly
stuffing his mouth.

STEPHEN SHIELDS

PIANOMAN

GERARD HANBERRY

Danny is at the piano. Comfortable. A wave for a group of middle-aged ladies around a table close by. They all smile back. This is his natural habitat. But tonight he will be less flirtatious. Orla, his partner, is at the bar. She rarely attends, not since the baby. Too much hassle.

Danny's fingers glide across the keys. Bluesy. Setting a mood. Aware of Orla's presence, long tanned legs , blond, like a famous model in a magazine. Lately, he feels less assured around her, sensing some new tilt in the relationship. Maybe the age difference. Who knows? For Danny these emotions are uncharted territory.

Two business types move in to chat her up.

"Sleazeballs," he mutters as he switches on the mike. "This next song's for my lovely lady sitting at the counter."

Orla twiddles her fingers at him but her smile is sour and she turns a little too abruptly back to her admirers.

The place begins to fill. Danny has to concentrate. He sings a few songs, plays an Elton John medley. When he checks again, she's gone from the bar. He slips a note. Damn! Where are the two sleazeballs? Missing. He sings "Leroy Brown" then takes a break.

He finds her in the lobby with Marge from the hair salon. Marge hates Danny. He took her home one night before he met Orla, said he would call. Didn't. Marge has a baby too. Same age as their Bryan. Orla got friendly with her in the maternity.

"Hi Danny!" says Marge, all sly smiles, "You on a break already?"

"Sorta. You ladies want a drink?"

"No, I'm fine," Orla replies. "Those two eejits bought me loads. Aren't lads awful thick, Marge?"

23

"Sure are." She didn't sound so convinced.

The three share a taxi home, dropping Marge off first. Orla is well gone. She sits in the back near the door, staring out the side window. Silent.

The flat smells of burnt toast and baby things. The sitter's boyfriend is there, looking happy.

"Bryan was no bother, never stirred." She takes the money. "Thanks Danny, call me anytime, no bother at all."

The boyfriend drops four empty Budweiser cans into the black refuse sack on the way out.

Danny spoons some instant into two mugs, clicks on the kettle. The lights go out.

"Shaggin' meter."

He fumbles for coins. When it comes back on Orla is sitting at the table just staring at the black toast crumbs scattered across the surface. He makes the coffee. Says nothing. She might cry or she might explode. This was never the plan.

When they first met Orla was a nineteen year-old student working part time in the hotel bar. Danny told her he was twenty-seven and single. He was actually ten years older and separated. They moved in together that summer, living on what Danny brought in playing seven nights a week and money put away from a stint in Grand Canaria. Wet Irish mornings spent in bed, sunny afternoons on the beach. On Orla's nights off he would finish as early as possible then rush back to the little flat - no hanging around chatting up tourists. They might watch a video, share a joint, fall into bed laughing. They laughed a lot that summer.

The night he said he loved her, he came clean about his age. She just laughed, called him a dirty old man. But then he told her about his wife in Dublin, that they still kept in touch. She became angry, said he should have told her. She cried and left the following day to stay with friends just back in town for the start of college. After three nights of torment he went and pleaded with her to come back. He was sorry, he'd been wrong, afraid she would not want him if she knew. Bryan was conceived that very afternoon.

Danny is wide awake, watching the dawn brighten through thin bedroom curtains. Something is brewing in Orla's head, maybe something nasty put there by Marge. They should be able to talk about it. Maybe today.

The baby starts to cry. Instantly Orla is out and on her feet, lifting him from the cot, whispering baby talk. She sits on the edge of the bed feeding him a bottle. The room is cramped, but at least the landlord is fine about it.

"Go and make another bottle Danny, I know you're awake."

When he returns, Bryan is back in his cot, Orla's eyes are closed. He puts a cold foot playfully against her leg.

"Grow up, Danny," she snaps, gathering the quilt around her.

He has heard these words before. Her parents used them when they arrived at the door all bluster, shouting, ordering her home. They would support her, their only daughter, they would raise the baby as their own. What about her studies? What future could she possibly have with a no-good, the likes of him? Their door would always be open to her when, and not if, things went wrong.

Orla is up tidying the flat when he comes back from the supermarket. She ignores his arrival.

"Look," he says at last," the sulks are no help. I'm doing my best …"

"Your best!" she yells, "If this is your best you're pathetic. We have no money, we live in a kip and you swan around as if you're God's gift. Well you're not … you're a joke …"

"I know things are a bit grim right now but …"

"Grim! What would you know. I have to stay in this dump every night while you chat up geriatrics in the residents' lounge. Don't think I don't know what you get up to …"

"You know that's not true. I bet that Marge has been saying things ..." But Orla is too angry to listen. Danny lets her rant on until at last Bryan wakes. She goes in to him, banging the bedroom door behind her. He has never seen her like this before.

Mary on reception calls Danny over when he arrives for work. "Phone message for you today. From the Canary Islands, if you don't mind. Wants you to ring straight away. What's the number worth to you Danny?"

"What ever your heart desires, my precious." Danny has to dig deep for his special smile. But it's worth it, Mary is special. "Put me through there, you sexy thing."

"You must be joking."

"Do it for me, babe."

"Pick up the phone in the lobby when it rings, you charmer."

Danny blows her a kiss.

"Hello, Riki here."

"Still poisoning the tourists Riki, or should I say Tommy, you big chancer?"

"Ah Danny Fingers! Still torturing the punters and fooling the señoritas I suppose?"

"Señoritas! Me? New leaf turned over, I've seen the light."

"Yeah? Well get your ass out here and see what a little light can do for the babes when they hit the sands. We're opening up The Beach Club again and you're the man we want."

Danny can't believe his ears. The old Beach Club, the night-life area in a huge, upmarket, self-catering compound. He had worked there before in the cabaret lounge, now Riki wants him as anchor man and entertainments manager, year round contract, good money, accommodation.

"Listen Riki, sounds great, but things are a little complicated at the moment."

"Don't tell me, let me guess. This wouldn't be a señorita type of complication, now would it?"

"And a little bambino one as well, Riki."

"Some new leaf you turned over, you canine, but hey, no problemo, bring them along if you want. Might cramp your style,

26

but there's plenty of room here at the apartments. I need a quick decision, Dan old son, call me tomorrow."

"Will do amigo, adios."

After the gig Danny sits alone at the counter in the resident's lounge thinking things through, still a bit rattled from the morning's uproar. But now, with the news about The Beach Club, things are sure to be fine again. Regular pay, sunshine, a paddling pool for Bryan when he gets a bit stronger, the world is turning to caress them both again. He might need to work a bit on his repertoire, add some crazy holiday songs. No big deal. Orla will be thrilled when he gets home, she deserves some good times. He leaves without finishing his drink.

The dark flat feels cold when he opens the door. Has Orla no coins for the meter? He switches on the light. It's as if the air has just settled back after some great upheaval.

"Orla!"

He checks the bedroom. Even Bryan's cot is gone.

TRIPTYCH

You hear me not
when I tell you the curve of your mouth
makes me smile at the sight
you turn and sigh, as I wordlessly utter your name
as if that makes it all right
as if the run of your fingers along my cheek
closes in on the distance you keep between us
as if the occasional meeting of eye
to eye makes up for an empty heart
as if the length of your body against mine
shuts out the silence
but how can it, when you hear me not?

***

I remember the day you left as if it were yesterday
and who's to say it wasn't?
It rained, and you stood there getting wet
but your blue eyes stayed dry; so blue
a clear day always reminds me of them
a ghost of a smile around your lips, a ghost of a promise
when you walked away, you never looked back
I remember that too.

***

In my dream of you, you look the same
except your eyes are warm
and your hands express, in motion
a language upon my body, without deceit
your mouth leaves a soundless train of truth along my skin
unspoken sentiments hold promise, not betrayal.
In my dream of you.

MISJA WEEJES

THE SNAKE PIT

Catriona Mitchell

When I entered the pub I recognised him straight away, although he looked less thuggish than I remembered. He was sitting in the far corner on a sofa, its upholstery a mosaic of cigarette scorches and chewing gum stains. A hulk of a man in a black leather jacket and polo neck, steroid-wide shoulders, skin a sickly orange tinge — as if he were compensating for the night-shifts with regular stints at the solarium.

They say if you work nights it shortens your life.

I propelled myself across the floor with a determination to see this through, however ugly. "Greg," I said, wondering if he'd recognise me. I had wound a silk scarf round my head like a turban, and was wearing loose-fitting jeans; he'd only ever seen me in stage make-up and lycra.

He looked up from his newspaper, took my hand, crushed it in his gargantuan one. "Jemima." He was wearing fat silver rings on two fingers and a thumb. His hand was hot; the metal was cool.

"Call me Mim," I said. "My parents called me Jemima for only one reason: to cause pain."

"They fuck you up, your Mum and Dad."

"Watch it, if you're going to recite poetry in here, you'd better be sure it's original." His glance followed mine to the bar, where a gaggle of drunken writer-types had gathered. I recognised one of them: he was a regular columnist for the paper.

"And then we do it too," Greg said.

"Do what?'

"Fuck people up." He smirked.

"Do you think you could say that a bit louder please?"

"Do I look like I come with a volume button?"

I glanced around the room, thankful there was no one near our table; it was still early. "I thought you were known for your discretion," I hissed.

"C'mon. You may look angelic, but I can see it a mile off, you're a wolf in sheep's clothing." He tilted his head backwards and bayed like a cartoon wolf at the moon.

I fixed him with a dark stare. His howls abated and he lifted up his hands in mock surrender. They were large as shovels, and the knuckles were battered and scarred.

"Whatever," he said. "How about I get us a drink?"

"A Bloody Mary for me. Easy on the Tabasco." I took a seat on the couch, only remembering at the last minute to say thanks.

Greg stood up. He looked artificially athletic and vital — like Action Man — next to the drinkers at the bar. Their faces were prematurely old, the skin capillaried like road maps. Hands like parrots' claws, clasped around pint glasses — as if that was what nature had intended them for.

Maybe I should have chosen a place where Greg would be less conspicuous, but at least here we wouldn't run into people we knew.

"I ordered you a sandwich," he said, coming back with my Bloody Mary and a pint of Guinness for himself. "Ham and cheese. Hungry?"

"No." I'd been off food for days, never felt so empty, but couldn't face a thing.

"You're much too skinny, you know. Turn sideways and you disappear altogether." He squashed back in on the sofa beside me. He smelled of something expensive, Hugo Boss maybe.

"I know. But I can't help it. Besides, I won't get paid to wobble on stage now will I?"

"Girl with your talent could get a job anywhere."

"Yeah, people are just bashing doors down to get a bald, embittered trapeze artist on their payroll."

"You know they adore you at The Snake Pit," he said. "Did you say bald?"

At that, I put my hands to my head and solemnly unwound the silk scarf, to reveal my bare, scorched scalp.

"Oh," he said. As he frowned his forehead wrinkled like a paper bag. He was too young to have so many wrinkles. "Oh."

I stared at the carpet, feeling unspeakably heavy. There was a long, pregnant pause.

"I saw you perform a few times," he said. "At The Snake Pit. I came inside on my breaks. You were terrific."

"Thanks," I mumbled.

"Added a touch of class to the place." His voice smacked of false cheer. "Especially that trick where you wound rope around your ankle, and dangled from the ceiling. How'd you learn to do that?"

"Bored in my bedroom as a teenager."

"Hmm. Ropes and hangings. Must have been a happy time."

The barmaid arrived at the table then, with my toasted sandwich. Her lips were fire-engine red to match her hair; she wore motorcycle boots and a snakeskin dress like a sheath. I wondered if she sloughed it would there be an identical one underneath.

"Mustard?" she asked, and as she made the 't', a bubble of spit arced from her scarlet gash of a mouth across the table, to settle on the top of Greg's pint. Time slowed down as I watched it, mesmerised. The grace of it. I've always been infatuated with movement.

"Mustard?" she all but screeched.

I started. "Yes, please."

"Darren! Mustard!" she shouted across the room, and a jar with a yellow plastic lid flew at her at breakneck speed. She caught it without moving or even blinking and slammed it down. "Here you go love." She set off on a dirty-glasses mission.

"Wow," said Greg, his gaze glued to her behind.

I sank back into the sofa. With my bald head and bruises, I felt far from feminine — more like a fledgling that had fallen from the nest and hadn't yet recovered from the shock. Seeing the barmaid only reminded me of my own ugliness.

I cleared my throat. I hadn't prepared what I wanted to say and now my tongue felt clumsy and foreign in my mouth. "Greg. Maybe we should talk about … you know… what we're here to talk about."

"Sure, anytime. Fire away."

"Well, I was told that … maybe …"

"That this was the kind of job I'm good for?" He grinned, displaying two rows of even if slightly yellowed teeth. It was an ugly subject we were circling, but he was sweet when he smiled.

I sighed. "Yes. I didn't want it to come to this. I wanted to play things straight, but no one would believe me. Not even the other girls. One of them even said, 'you should be so lucky'. *You should be so lucky.*"

"So what's the story?"

He sounded so flip, a burst of irritation surged through me and helped me find my tongue. "Well Greg, maybe you should take another look at my head. Contrary to what you might think, I did not do this for reasons of pleasure. Or vanity. You might recall, I once had hair."

Greg nodded. "Sure. You wore it in a plait, long as my arm. Nice chestnut colour."

"Julian didn't think so."

"Who?"

"The flame-thrower. Works at The Snake Pit, prancing around the stage in a Chinese satin gown and a mask, being a dragon, breathing fire?"

"Yeah, I remember the guy. Good-looking. Thick-set."

"Yes."

"Thick, too."

"You got the one."

"He your boyfriend?"

"No." I hesitated. "Not after this, what do you think?"

"What'd he do to you?"

My bottom lip started to tremble violently, as if I were a shaky house with an earthquake coming. I expected the glasses to start rattling on the tables, the walls to cave in, at any moment.

Greg peered at me. His eyes were a murky green close up, not grey as I'd thought.

"He ..." lunging for my Bloody Mary, I knocked it over by mistake.

"On second thoughts, don't say it. I don't need to know."

I chewed my lip, and rubbed tomato juice into my jeans, hoping the stain wouldn't show. My stomach roared like a caged beast.

"You really should eat something," he said, moving the sandwich towards me. The orange cheddar had coagulated into fleshy lumps. "Preferably not part of your own anatomy."

My stomach lurched at the sight of the food and I pushed the plate away. "Suffice to say," I said unsteadily, "Julian has an infatuation with flames. As a teenager he used to set fire to his neighbours' hedges. "

"He told you that?"

"Yeah. When he was drunk."

"Whatever turns you on."

I ran my hand over my scalp, protectively. "Greg, teach him a lesson for me, will you?"

"I don't know."

"You said you'd help."

"I said I *might*. I'll think about it. But you know Mim, I'm beginning to see, violence only begets violence."

"What?" I was exasperated. Maybe I knew he was right, but it wasn't what I wanted to hear, not at all. "What the fuck are you talking about? You're the one does this for a living."

"Yeah, but I changed my mind. About you, I mean."

"Huh?"

"You're OK. You don't want to mess with this, it's too ugly for you."

"No, *I'm* the one that's too ugly. Look at me! It's not as if I had a lot going for me before, but look at me now!"

"You're not *that* bad."

"Oh thanks, I feel much better now."

"I mean ..."

"Look, save your empathy, it's very noble and all, but it isn't exactly helping. I need you to give Julian a scare. A warning. Make him sorry for what he's done. He's humiliated me. *Ruined* me. And I want to be sure he won't do the same again, to me or anyone else."

Greg strummed his fingers on the table awhile, frowning, then turned to look at me. "OK. So have it your way. When?"

How fickle men were, I thought nastily. "Well that was quick. Boy you really stick to your guns. What is it, need the cash? Expensive after-shave habit to feed?"

He wasn't amused.

"Anytime. Saturday, maybe." I lit a cigarette. "The club closes at four. He'll probably hail a cab around four-thirty."

"And how d'you want this handled?"

"With fists I presume."

"Not necessarily."

"What, you've got a smorgasbord of violent means I can choose from? What's on the menu this week, big boy?"

"That's up to you, Jemima." His voice was icy.

"Mim."

"Whatever."

"Just wipe that smug smile off his face for a while. I don't care how."

Greg stood up. "I'll need clear instructions. Have a think about your ways and means, while I do something about this thirst of mine."

"Make mine a double, would you?" I shouted after him.

To entertain myself in his absence I opened his newspaper and flicked through, hoping to find the Gary Larson cartoon. But a wiry builder in a white singlet and cement-caked boots sat on the sofa next to me, and put his pint on the paper, preventing me from turning the page. He was trouble, I knew it straight away.

"That seat's taken," I said. He leaned in towards me.

"You're fookin beautiful, you know that?" His breath stank of beer and his eyes were glassy like those of a long-dead fish.

I ignored him and tried to read my horoscope. *You only get one crack at real love*, it said.

He leaned closer. "You deaf or wha?"

Expect a change in your romantic affairs by the end of the day.

"What you reading for?"

"What am I reading *for?*"

A shadow fell across the page. It was Greg, blocking the light with his bulk. Scowling, he grabbed the builder by the shoulder and I feared a sharp, violent outburst. But Greg's expression quickly changed to one of surprise.

"Oh, hey man," he said. "Donal?"

"Yeah. So?"

Greg smiled, an affectionate, tender smile I hadn't seen on him before. It took years off him. "It's me, Greg Keany."

The two had lived next door to each other when they were at school, and hadn't seen each other since.

Greg went off to find a spare bar stool, leaving me to contend with this unforeseen addition to the table. Donal was effeminate, if you looked beyond the biceps and the work-boots — he had a slender, fine-boned face, shapely lips, long eyelashes several shades darker than his hair. But his features clashed with his demeanour. He was full of violence and rage; his cold, narrowed eyes betrayed it, and he sat tense on his seat like a puma, ready to pounce. Ready to kill.

"So, Donal," I said, after an awkward pause. "What brings you to The Black Rose?"

"The fookin art gallery in here. What do you think?"

I glanced up at the walls. A crude acrylic painting of a toilet roll stared back at me. A price tag next to it said 450 euro.

"Hey man, what are you doing with yourself now?" asked Greg, back with a stool in his hand.

"Working on the sites," Donal mumbled.

Greg sat down and took a swig of his pint. "Do you enjoy it? Does it pay you well?" His tone was avuncular.

"'s OK."

"I always thought you were going to be an actor. You were brilliant, you should be on the telly."

Donal froze, and the veins stood out on his arms and neck. His frame turned as rigid as scaffolding. "I'll fookin kill yeh," he shouted. He stood up from his stool and sat down, stood up and sat down again, and white froth gathered at the sides of his mouth like scum on a polluted stream. "You're not listening to me. You're just like the fookin rest of them, trying to tell me what to do ..."

"Hey, cool down."

"Fuck you. I don't listen to anyone, d'ye hear me? Do ye?"

Greg didn't respond this time, but kept his face implacable, and Donal quietened. "How d'ye stay so calm, man?" he asked after a moment. "Don't you feel that fookin *force*?"

"Do you know what I do now, Donal? I do Yoga," said Greg. That caught my attention. "Yoga?"

"I learned it inside."

I burst out laughing. "You go to prison for cutting a man's finger off and get Yoga lessons as punishment?"

"Something like that," Greg said.

This was outrageous. "Let me get this straight," I said. "They let you out, you go back to hurting people for a living. Only difference is, these days you do Yoga to calm yourself when you get up in the mornings."

"Yeah, I may still be a brute, but I feel *so* much better about myself as a person." It took me a while to realise he was teasing me now. "Well that's good to know," I said, sinking sulkily into the sofa.

"But really, I'm getting away from the night work," Greg said. "I've had enough. I'm getting clean."

"Not now you don't," I said.

"Soon. I've been training to teach Power Yoga. My mate wants me to give classes at his health club. Loads of cash in it. Chicks too."

Donal's head had been going between us like a ping pong ball. "But what does this yoghurt shit have to do with anything, man? What about the fookin force?"

"What force?" I wanted to know.

Donal turned to me. "You wouldn't fookin understand," he spat. "Women will never understand men. Never. You hear me! Never. So don't even try."

"OK. *OK!*"

"All that shite about men needing their female side... They all want to make us into poofters or something. Bollocks!" He looked to Greg for support, who merely shrugged. Donal fixed his snake-like eyes back on me — the pupils had all but vanished. "I don't need a fookin feminine side. We're different. Men and women are *different.*"

"Sure. Of course," I said, to assuage him. "Of course." He was beginning to scare me, and yet hooked into the conversation, I felt compelled to go on. "That talk about the feminine side just means you're meant to have feelings, to have a heart," I said, as gingerly as if I'd been stepping out onto a frozen lake.

The ice cracked with the sound of a gunshot. Donal slammed his fist on the table, upsetting the drinks. The glasses smashed; tomato juice, lemon slices and jagged shards flew onto the carpet.

"I don't need fookin feelings," Donal shouted. "I don't need a fookin heart. Men don't need that shite. Men need to feel the fookin *force.*" And he balled up his fists again and held them up to his chin as if preparing for a fight.

"Women can be violent too, you know," I fired.

Donal jumped at my words, recoiling like he'd been stung. His mouth flapped open and closed like a door slamming in a windstorm. I looked at him, unblinking, and after a while he muttered something unintelligible, stood up, steadying himself on the table, and staggered off in the direction of the men's room.

"Enough. Can we please get rid of him now? " I said to Greg.

"Not yet. I want to talk to him."

"You and I have things to discuss. Important things."

"This is important too. It's doing me good to be reminded of who I was, once. I haven't seen Donal since I was ..." He counted on his thick bratwurst-fingers. "Eleven."

He stopped speaking as Donal returned with a fresh pint of beer and a whisky chaser. The silence between us became palpable. Guiltily, I searched for something to say.

"Did a bird shit on your jeans?" Highbrow stuff I know, but I was getting a little drunk.

"No it did *not*," Donal said, and started scraping away at the yellow crust on his trousers. "You know what that is?"

I shrugged.

"D'ye want to know what that is?" There was pent-up rage in his voice again. "I'll tell you what that is. Ever heard of cavity filler? Look." He scraped with his fingernail. The sandy residue clung stubbornly to the denim. "When you're building, right, you cement a wall in. Sometimes there's still gaps, so you use this stuff called cavity filler. Right?"

"Uh-huh."

"RIGHT, Greg?" He wanted to be sure he had our full attention.

Greg nodded.

"It comes in a can. A spray can. You hold the nozzle up to the gap and you spray, right? It dries solid within a couple of minutes. It dries hard as stone."

He looked us both in the eye again. I dreaded what was coming next.

"Well I was working in Holland, right. In Rotterdam. With my brother Liam and these three guys from Cavan. And d'ye know what those Dutch bastards did? DO YOU KNOW WHAT THOSE DUTCH BASTARDS DID?"

He was shouting at the top of his voice. The barman glanced over, annoyed. Greg put a hand on Donal's arm. He shook it off.

"One night, right ..." He broke off and for a moment I thought he was going to weep. "One night, they'd been drinking. And they cornered these three Irish guys, young guys they were, and my brother Liam, and they tied them up. They beat them. And then they pulled down their pants and shoved the nozzle of the cavity-filler up their holes." He was shaking. "And ... they sprayed it. They sprayed it up them until their insides were full of it." He grabbed my hand violently. "Feel it. FEEL IT!" he cried, rubbing my fingers against the stuff. It was coarse and scratchy, like sandpaper. "Feel how hard it is. Can you imagine having that inside you? Up to your stomach."

He was teary now.

"Oh my God," I said.

We were all silent. Donal had his head in his hands.

"Did they die?" Greg asked in a hoarse voice. He'd been listening intently; now the colour seemed to have drained from behind his pseudo-tan.

"Course they fookin died. Course they fookin did."

"Pretzels, anyone? Fresh pretzels!" A plump blonde in white shorts, sporting a gingham-covered basket, was making her way through the tables.

"Not Liam," said Greg.

"Yeah." It was barely a whisper.

Though shaken, Greg took command of the situation. He bought Donal a pretzel — anything to change the subject, lift the mood. The tactic worked: Donal, distracted, snapped out of his misery. "What the fook's that?" he asked, picking up the pretzel, examining it up close, screwing up his entire face in bewilderment and wonder.

"It's a German roll," said Greg. "Eat it. It'll do you good. Soak up the alcohol."

"It … It looks like one of dem plastic dog turds. Where's the fookin nutritional value in that? Huh? Answer me that. Where's the fookin ham?"

And then he stood up and started to shout. "Give me pig. GIVE ME PIG!"

"Sit down!" Greg ordered. Donal sat.

"I'm going to kill a fookin pig tonight. Ye want to come with me?"

"Shut up," said Greg.

"Why not? You scared? I got the equipment."

"I don't want to get put inside again," said Greg. "And neither, for that matter, do you."

"I've got to do *something*. Either I kill a pig or I kill myself." Rage was trying to leap out of him, through his skin.

Greg changed the subject, to talk of the good old days: a safe bet. "I remember ... I remember when your sister Siobhan used to want to hang around with us, only we wouldn't let her."

"Yeah," Donal grinned. He relaxed visibly. The tension dropped from his shoulders.

"And I remember that dog you had, what was it, a labrador?"

"A labrador *retriever*," Donal corrected him.

"And I remember that wheelbarrow we had. That was fun. I used to push your little brother Stephen around ..."

Donal stiffened. Spat on the carpet. Turned purple with rage. "You push my little brother around, man, I'll fookin KILL YEH!" And he leapt for Greg's throat.

I froze, petrified.

Greg's face flushed red and his eyes bulged as they stared directly into Donal's, just inches away. With lightning speed Greg wrenched the smaller man's hands off his neck, coughed, drew himself up to his full size, like a lizard that expands its neck-frills to scare the enemy, and put his hands around Donal's skinny throat. He started to squeeze, and I thought I heard something snap. Beads of sweat stood out on Donal's forehead like sequins; his eyes darted fearfully from side to side.

But then Greg moaned like a wounded beast, and looked terribly sad. He threw Donal to the ground. "Fuck this. Fuck the lot of you," he cried, slumping onto the sofa with an air of pure dejection. Although he was staring down at the carpet I could have sworn he had tears in his eyes.

Donal pulled himself up by the table-leg and sat rubbing his neck with a sullen expression, then stared into his beer as if it held the key to the universe. None of us spoke. Finally Greg lifted his head, nodded at me, and rose with dignity. "We're going to go now, Donal." His voice was low, and unnaturally level; it scared me.

Donal continued to stare into his pint, as if he hadn't heard. Greg tried to take his hand to shake it, but the gesture was refused.

"I'm sorry to hear about your brother, man."

No response.

Greg and I walked to the door. I hadn't realised how drunk I was, and swayed a little, my sight blurry. I clutched at Greg's leather-clad arm for support.

"Do you think he'll be OK?" I asked, as soon as we were out in the bitter night air.

"Who knows," he said dully.

"Poor guy." I meant it too; I *was* sorry for Donal's pain — and yet the conversation had given me an idea, like the flash from a lighthouse on a foggy night, offering hope to a lost ship. I gave Greg a moment to collect himself before voicing my thoughts.

"Greg?"

"Yeah?"

"I know that upset you. But his story gave me an answer to your question."

"What question?"

"You said I could choose."

"Choose what? What are you on about?"

"Julian. He who plays with fire. Remember?"

Greg's face twisted into an ugly shape. "Get out of here."

"What, you don't want the job now?"

"No, Mim. I don't. Just forget it."

The weariness in his voice startled me. "Fine," I snapped. "Fine. If you don't do it, then I'll ask someone who will." I turned on my heel, though neither as quickly nor as dramatically as I would have liked.

To my chagrin Greg made no move to stop me. I cast an eye over my shoulder and saw him walking away, slowly, hands in pockets, head lowered in resignation. He was no longer a hulk of a man; but a fraction of his former size.

When I re-entered the pub I saw Donal straight away, exactly where we'd left him. He was sitting in the far corner, on the green sofa, its velvet upholstery a mosaic of cigarette scorches and chewing gum stains. I propelled myself across the floor with a determination to see this through, however ugly.

TONGUE TIED

If you ask me once more
if I'd like a cup of tea
I'll scream.

I'll scream so loud
that my tonsils
or what remains of them

will stick to a tree
at the other side of the road
and my tongue

will sit nicely
at the edge of Fenit pier
floodlit by night

and the sound of my scream
will hollow a hole
in the ocean bed

big enough for the two of us
and maybe then you'll know
it's not tea I'm after

MARION MOYNIHAN

CAT AND MOUSE

I can identify with the mouse
I know what it's like to be swallowed whole.

Maybe swallowed whole is too strong
I saw him eat the head first.
He left the gallbladder,
the bile, the bitter taste.

He is a house cat
he sleeps on my bed every night.

MARION MOYNIHAN

MY MOTHER'S DIARY

I found a small red diary in your drawer.

> *Changed the sheets today, cleaned the sitting room,*
> *Ann and Frank called, had a bath, Teresa phoned,*
> *Went to the grave, paid ESB, pains bad.*

I was writing in *my* journal when the phone rang the morning
you died.

> *Dear God, I haven't written for a few days because I was in a*
> *bad state. I think I may have been angry at you, God, for*
> *taking away the man I love. I threatened to take some tablets at*
> *the weekend, if the pain got bad enough, but I didn't have the*
> *courage. I think I may have frightened my friends though.*
> *(18th March 2002)*

I left for the hospital not knowing that you were already dead.

We had the same doctor, he told me once
that the difference between us
was that *I* knew I was fucked up, you didn't.

I'm driving around in your car, I haven't washed it in weeks.
You had four thousand miles on the clock in three years,
I have eighteen thousand in nine months.
I wear the wedding ring that never came off your finger
until the pains got so bad they had to force it off.
I use your umbrella everyday.

I wish all the things you told me
had been written into your diary.
But then, a diary the size of a prayer book
couldn't contain all that anger…

I don't have to spend a week
psyching myself up to phone you anymore
or take deep breaths, counting to ten
before arriving at your door.
Now I say, *thank you Kit*, when I'm driving through
Bearna, Spiddal, Lettermore, Lettermullen.
Fucked up or not, I'm doing fine.

MARION MOYNIHAN

MY SON'S BANANA SUIT

On the subway
between Sunnyside in Queens
and the French restaurant
in Times Square
you told me
how much you hated it,
that you called it
your *banana suit*.

Your forced laugh
echoed through tunnels
under the Hudson river
into the homes of people
who never saw you
in that canary yellow suit.

Just before Grand Central,
I saw your eyes framed
with my father's dark brows,
your forehead furrowed and deep,
as you told me about the day
you discovered your father and your brother gone,
how, for the last ten years you've blamed me.

As far as you were concerned,
I might as well have died.

I got it wrong like the *banana suit*,
foolishly thinking that in not telling you the truth
I was protecting you.

MARION MOYNIHAN

NIGHTSWIMMING

Benjamin Coombs

Steve is my best friend. We met at juniors and were in the same class all through school. We got arrested for shoplifting together, kissed our first girls behind the sports centre, and even coughed and spluttered through our first joint together. The thing is that we're different. I've always been sensitive and dreamy, but Steve is practical and scientific; he gets on with life rather than worrying about it. We look alike though, and people always assume we're brothers.

We lost contact when we hit eighteen and went off to different universities, but when we hooked up again four years later, our friendship was stronger than ever. I was amazed at how much he'd changed. He'd learned to play the piano, was reading Castaneda and Hesse, and started dressing in smoky cords and Salvation Army cardigans. He'd also grown a goatee, which he would finger thoughtfully as we talked about the meaning of the universe at 3 o'clock in the morning. I couldn't believe it; I felt like John Major had turned into Jimi Hendrix when I was looking the other way.

It was around this time that he met Niamh, and in no time at all they were inseparable. She was a cracking girl, with sparkling blue eyes and a shock of wayward brown curls, who was perpetually smiling. They were a perfect match, and I'd never seen Steve so happy. What amazed me was that their partnership remained fragrant and shiny, like an orchard after the rain, even a couple of years down the line together. I wondered what the secret was.

They found this gorgeous little place in Brighton, and even though neither of them worked full time the bank came up trumps.

Steve couldn't believe it — said it made him a feel like a grown-up at last. He found work subbing at the local newspaper and Niamh commuted up to the city to do production work at Capitol. She was trying her hand at painting and sculpting too, so they turned the basement into a studio. She had a real knack for it, and started spending a lot of her free time down there.

The first time I visited, she refused to let me in, saying there was nothing worth seeing. Eventually I persuaded her, and when I stepped inside I was especially drawn to one picture of a boy sitting under the branches of a huge oak. The leaves seemed to sway as if in a gentle breeze, so imbued with life were they, and the boy's face was incredibly beautiful — it took my breath away.

"That's fucking amazing!" I told her " I can't believe you did that"

She stared down at her toes.

"Oh it needs a lot of work — I couldn't get the colours right — I didn't have time to finish it off properly."

Steve laughed and put his arm around her. "You can't give her a compliment. She dodges them like a pro. She's got no idea how amazing she is." Niamh looked embarrassed, but a smile opened out across her face.

I'd go to see them as often as I could, and the three of us would stay up all night watching old movies or talking and listening to music. They radiated contentment and I was happy for them. To me they were proof that happy endings were not just something out of a crappy movie; that it really was possible to find a soul mate. When everything turned to shit for them, it knocked me for six.

I got the phonecall at midnight one Saturday, had a sinking feeling as soon as the phone rang. It was Niamh's mother telling me there had been an accident, and the next thing I knew I was frantically scribbling down the address of some hospital. It turned out that Niamh had slipped and fallen off the edge of the curb on the way back from the pub. It was an innocuous looking fall, but she'd stayed down and never moved. I got into the car and drove down there in a daze, and when I arrived I found Steve pacing up and down the corridors like a sentry on speed. He was pale, and his face was a mask of worry; it hurt me to see him like that. Suddenly, I couldn't think of anything to say, and it was Steve who broke the silence, speaking softly as if there was a vast distance between him and his own voice.

"They've been doing scans and stuff — the doctor said we won't know for a couple of days. Said we have to be patient."

I nodded, wondering if I should hug him, but feeling awkward and hesitant. I struggled to think of the right thing to say, and when the words came out, they sounded stupid.

"It'll be alright," I managed. "She's a tough cookie."

He shook his head. "She was right next to me — I had my arm around her — and then the next second, she slipped away from me. It didn't seem like anything … I was laughing, for fuck's sake, but she just lay there …"

I went closer, and put one arm around him. "She's in good hands. She'll be back home before you know it."

The smell of the hospital made me uneasy, filling me with a curious sense of dread. I waited with him anxiously, feeling scared and uncomfortable. Every so often I trudged off to the vending machine for chocolate, which I ate hurriedly without even tasting it. Steve was chain-smoking rollups, and when I tried to talk to him, to reassure him, he didn't hear me. He was lost inside his own mind, navigating a maze of fear; all I could do was be with him.

The last time we'd sat around forlornly like this was when my kid brother got pneumonia, years before. It had been touch and go for a while; the poor little sod had even turned blue. Steve had stayed with me. He'd brought flapjacks and tea cakes crammed into see-through lunch boxes, and a flask of strong sweet coffee with Jamesons in it. Now it was my turn, only this time there was no whisky to drive out the cold.

They eventually let us in to see Niamh three days after the accident. When we entered I couldn't help thinking that she looked beautiful, propped up in bed primly in a starched white gown, smiling gently amidst an oasis of flowers and miniature teddy bears. Niamh said hello and Steve began sobbing like a baby. I felt a bit awkward, like a voyeur or something. A couple of minutes later the doctor charged in brusquely and perched himself on the end of the bed.

"We were worried initially," he said. "But I'm happy to tell you that the scans show no signs of permanent damage. We're going to keep you in for a further forty-eight hours, but after that, there's no reason why you can't go home."

Niamh looked at him as if he were her very own angel, and he smiled back. We all thanked him profusely, but he hurried off, overwhelmed by our gratitude.

When Niamh got out of the hospital she spent a fortnight taking it easy, but nothing could prevent her from returning to work. She bounced back so quickly that we almost forgot the whole episode. At first she only did three days a week, but after a couple of months they let her back full time. Steve went around the whole time smiling, relieved that the nightmare was over.

All that changed the Friday before Easter. Niamh was standing quietly in a checkout line at Tescos, cradling avocados and a bottle of Chilean red, when she had a brain seizure and collapsed. The ambulance men were there inside four minutes, and found her sprawled on the floor below a row of shiny chocolate bars. There was nothing they could do.

The doctors couldn't explain it, and I know that her father met with solicitors to discuss a lawsuit, but little came of it. Nothing could bring her back to us anyway.

The strange thing is that Steve was a rock in the days that followed. He cooperated with her parents making arrangements for the funeral, phoning friends and relatives, taking care of the thousand little jobs that descend in the aftermath. All the time he reminded us how her life was full of joy, how she would have wanted us to celebrate her life rather than wallow in tears. I was gob-smacked, felt awed and proud to see the way that the crisis brought out the best in him. It was only a few weeks later, after the funeral was over, that he crumbled. He sank beneath layers of anger and despair, until he couldn't see the point in getting out of bed anymore.

He left the newspaper he was working at and moved out of the house in Brighton, saying she was everywhere in there. He moved up to Lewisham, into a pokey little flat next to a video store, and grew a Jim Morrison beard. He started to smoke dope all day and watch TV with the curtains drawn. He had lots of support from the friends and family around him, but it wasn't enough, and that left us feeling helpless.

The scariest thing of all though, was his anger. He'd always been a gentle soul who hated confrontation, so when he started to get aggressive it totally freaked us out. The first episode was when I coaxed him into coming out to a club with me — the first time he'd had a proper night out in the six months since Niamh's death. It was a seventies theme night and everything went smoothly to begin with, I got him a couple of tequilas to liven him up, and even managed to drag him onto the dancefloor. He was bobbing his head along to the Jackson 5 when I left to get more drinks, but then at the bar I got sidetracked by a West Indian girl.

When I eventually fought my way back through the throng, I arrived just in time to see Steve standing toe to toe with this guy, screaming abuse at him. Before I could do anything, Steve had taken a wild swing, and the next thing he was on top of the guy, pounding his face in. I looked on in horror. One girl was screaming, whilst others backed away to try to avoid the mess as three bouncers piled in, the biggest one pulling Steve off by his hair. They dragged him out through the crowd, and I dashed after them as fast as I could. When I stepped onto the street, I found him lying on his side bleeding into a puddle, and for a moment the whole episode seemed so unreal that my mind refused to work properly.

I tried to clean him up, but even then he looked such a mess that none of the taxis would take us, until one kindly old cabbie took pity, and helped me drag him into the back. The next day Steve wouldn't talk about it, and refused to say what the guy had done to make him so angry. He tried to make out that it was just the drink.

We were all so worried that it really took its toll, and his mum especially became greyer and greyer and started to look really old and worn. It was a tremendous relief when she tracked down a counsellor for Steve.

John was a funny wee man with bright brown eyes and long wispy hair, and a silver hoop in one ear. He had a penchant for purple corduroy trousers and an infectious laugh. We had to coerce Steve into the sessions with him at the start, but eventually they clicked, and settled into the routine of meeting twice a week. Steve kept quiet about the whole process. It was hard for me to stand on the sidelines and watch, and I resented the fact that a stranger could help him more than I could. Eventually, he started working again, writing for a food magazine, and he emerged again into the big scary world to visit friends and go to the pub and cinema. It seemed that he was over the worst.

He'd come over to my flat after work and we'd hang out together, watching foreign movies and playing pool on my crappy little table. It was nice, but it wasn't like it used to be. He'd never pile eagerly into my records or reach over to strum the guitar, and I missed the heartfelt conversations that would spill over into the early hours. One night he told me about his plans to go to India to see the Himalayas, and I had the uneasy feeling that he was saying it all for my benefit. It was as if he was trying to cover over a great chasm of apathy. For all I knew this was normal, perhaps it took years to get the spark back after a trauma, but what scared me was the thought that it would never come back. On bad days I had the urge to track down a couple of hospital paddles and hook them up to the mains, plaster them to his chest to kick start him into life. Anything to get the blood firing again.

At the beginning of spring I felt fed up. I was desperate to shake things up a bit. I hit upon a plan of taking Steve away for a weekend to Galway, hoping it might inject a bit of excitement into him. I got on to the Internet and booked the flights straight away, without even checking with him. When I told him he was totally nonplussed, but I badgered him until he agreed to come. The cynic in my head nagged at me, told me I was wasting my time, but I needed to hope. Besides, I had an ulterior motive; I was keen to catch up with this girl called Sarah, whom I'd lost contact with since she'd moved to Galway.

When I phoned her she said she'd love to see me, even offered to put us both up. On the flight out I felt excited. Something about Ireland had always fired my imagination. Steve had never been there before, but all he did during the journey was moan about the lack of legroom.

Sarah was waiting outside the terminal when we got there, smiling. She looked scruffily pretty in a flowing red skirt and green knitted jumper, with rings and beads jangling at her wrists. Her blonde hair flew out behind her as she walked toward me.

"I knew the dreaded day would come," she said, her blue eyes full of mischief. She hugged Steve hello too, and then we jumped into her decrepit silver Talbot and headed for the city. I didn't notice the road or the scenery during the drive; I was too busy catching up and sharing my news with Sarah, who was in great form. Steve just stared out of the window most of the time. It seemed like only a few minutes passed before we arrived in Galway, where Sarah had a place in the centre of town.

Her flat was beautiful. It overlooked the river, with a balcony to savour the view from. Inside, there were wooden furnishings and colourful eastern wall hangings, with green plants flowing over in every nook and cranny. I felt right at home. We dumped our bags and went for fish and chips at McDonagh's, and then made straight for the local boozer. It was only 3 o'clock in the afternoon, but we thought we'd get into the swing of things.

We huddled together in a cosy little corner of the pub, drinking endless Guinness and Bushmills and soaking up the warm atmosphere. As the day went on Sarah introduced us to more and more of her friends; she seemed to know every other person in the place. A group of musicians arrived for the evening session, and amidst the laughter and the strains of the mandolin and fiddle Steve perked up a bit. He still lapsed occasionally into awkward silences, but at least we got some conversation out of him. When he went to grab a burger, Sarah and I talked about what had happened to him.

"You can tell he's not right," she said.

"I know," I said, "but he's so much better than he was."

"There must be something we can do," she said, and her voice was tight with concern. When Steve got back he told us he was feeling knackered, and we all agreed that it was time to hit the sack. As we staggered home, Sarah seemed thoughtful.

I overslept the next morning and Sarah had been out already by the time I stumbled downstairs with a throbbing head. Now she was busying herself in the kitchen, humming. She put a mug of coffee into my hand as I shuffled in.

"You look like you need perking up," she said. She leaned forward then and kissed me feather soft on the lips, then laughed at the shock on my face.

"It's going to be a beautiful day!" she said. The spitting of fat and the smell of burning bacon broke the spell, and she turned to rescue breakfast. I crumpled into one of the chairs at the little wooden table, struggling to fight through the fog in my brain. Steve appeared then, plonked himself down opposite me and unfurled the paper.

"Hey," I said to him. "I feel like going exploring today."

"You haven't got time to go off gallivanting," said Sarah. "We're going for a drive after breakfast, and you'll need jumpers and waterproofs."

I looked incredulously over at Steve, but he just shrugged. I opened my mouth to complain but she put her finger to her lips and walked away.

It took a while to get out of town, but soon we were out on the open road, cruising along winding country lanes and over bare grey hills. Sunlight streamed in through the windows and I savoured the contours and colour of the Burren landscape, with its gnarled grey rocks carved by the elements. It was unusual, like the surface of the moon. I asked her where we were headed.

"It's a surprise."

An hour later, as we wound around narrow coast roads, the weather shifted. It was as if a towering black bird had spread her wings and blocked out the sun. We were surrounded by thick blankets of cloud, and the omens did not look good. A few moments later, we pulled up on the side of the road just as the rain began to pour down. Sarah jumped out and fumbled around in the back of the car, pulling out three bulky green rucksacks.

"Here you go," she said plonking them down in front of us. "One each."

We walked along the road for about five hundred yards and then Sarah ducked under a barbed wire fence and trudged down across the muddy field towards the open expanse of the sea. Then we followed a narrow path along the top of a low cliff. The ground was wet and muddy and the track weaved over crumbling walls, between clumps of blackberry and massive grey rocks. I kept my eyes glued to the track, and didn't look up.

A few minutes later, as we turned around the cliff face, I was surprised to see a middle-aged woman sitting on the rocks in a gigantic yellow oilskin. She waved at us, and then turned back, peering down into the ocean. I followed her gaze across the horseshoe bay, but saw nothing special.

"Is there coral down there?" I asked her.

"No," she said. "I'm waiting for Mara."

"Who's Mara?" I asked.

At that moment I heard Sarah let out a squeal of excitement. Then I heard Steve's voice, "Holy fuck."

I turned around to see a large grey dolphin arcing up out of the water and disappearing into the heavy swell. It was magnificent. The German woman, Birgit, flashed a conspiratorial smile.

"You'd better put on your wet suit!" she said.

We grappled with our wetsuits and then scrambled towards the ocean over impossibly smooth, slippy rock. The tide was coming in all the time and the wind whipped up big waves, which pounded the great grey ring of stone. I felt intimidated by the wild power of the ocean, but I pushed past my fear and slipped down the rocks into the water. Steve and Sarah were ahead of me, paddling eagerly out to the dolphin.

In my suit I found I could ride the swell effortlessly, which was a tremendous feeling of freedom. As I scanned the water for the telltale grey fin, I was surprised that I no longer felt fear, only anticipation. Then I sensed something moving below me, and I looked down to see the body of the dolphin. I felt her rubbery body brushing against my toe tips, and I watched as she moved lithely through the water. I called out, shouting into the air, full of childish wonder. I followed her closely as she streaked over towards Steve and Sarah, swimming as fast as I could. The dolphin reached them just as a big wave surged over them, and with a flick of her tail she threw herself forward and across, riding the wave like a surfer.

Steve was throwing himself around in the water idiotically, all the time calling, "come on girl". He was completely unselfconscious.

For the first few minutes she came quite close, but she wouldn't let us touch her. Gradually though, she became friendlier, brushing closer and closer, and letting us caress her all along her body. She was powerful and masterful in the water, and yet she was infinitely gentle when she was close to us. We were all giggling uncontrollably at the sheer delight of it, and we knew that the dolphin was enjoying it as much as we were. At one point she actually stopped swimming and rolled over onto her back beside Steve, letting him tickle her belly.

He wanted to get a glimpse of her properly under the water so he pulled down his mask and got the snorkel ready. Then he put his face down in the water, turning in circles, searching her out. After a while he surfaced again, roaring at the top of his lungs.

By now the sun was going down, and above the horizon the first stars were emerging. We had no desire to get out though, and in the twilight the movement of the dolphin in the water close to us took on a dreamlike quality. It felt like it was just the four of us, playing eternally, and nothing else existed.

When it was dark, we decided that it was time to go, though we all felt like staying forever. It was a struggle to get back on to solid ground because the waves pushed us up against the rocks and there was only a narrow cleft in the stone. Somehow we managed it, and huddled together up on the rocks, shivering. We hadn't noticed while we were in the water, but now we were freezing.

We hurried to dry off, the wind whistling around us, and the three of us sharing the joy of it. We talked rapidly and breathlessly, the energy pouring off us, as the moon came up solemnly on the horizon. I asked Steve what had happened when he put his head under, and he looked at me with eyes full of awe.

"I saw her fin swimming toward me so I put my head under and waited. The water was murky and all I could see was a few strands of seaweed, so I almost gave up. Suddenly I saw her coming out of the gloom, swimming along the bottom, and I looked right into her eyes. She came close to me and then we turned in an arc together, looking at each other all the time. I felt like she really *saw* me. Something ... "

He trailed off, unable to find the words. To hear him talking like that, to see the childlike wonder in his eyes, made me feel incredibly blessed, incredibly grateful.

In the car on the way back to the city, we all sat quietly, savouring the warm glow that the day had left with us. I was thinking about the journey back to England, wishing that our adventure didn't have to end so soon. I fell asleep then, and awoke as we arrived back in Galway.

That night Sarah and I talked until morning, and she agreed to come over to London for a visit in the summer. Our farewell at the airport the next day was still gut wrenching, but it was easier now that I knew I would see her again soon.

When I got back home the experience with the dolphin stayed with me. I was on a massive high for about six days, and even after that I felt permeated by a gentle sense of well being unlike anything I had felt before. I knew Steve felt it too.

A fortnight after we got back, he joined this drumming club at his local community centre, and was meeting new people all the time. He also started writing again. He dug his dad's dusty old typewriter out from amongst the boxes in the loft, and was driving his neighbours mad with the clackety-clack of the keys into the early hours. He loved the thing, especially the swoosh as you changed onto another line, and the little bell; said it reminded him of being on a bicycle when he was kid.

Everything looked like it was going great for him, but my only concern was that he had never talked about Niamh; he just avoided the subject completely. I longed for him to open up and talk about how he was feeling, but it wasn't my place to force him.

Then, three months after we got back, Steve decided to have a big clear out and chuck away a lot of his old stuff. I was a natural hoarder myself, and I admired the ruthless way he went about it. We hauled countless boxes over to the charity shop and I got some nice goodies out of it too, like his sheepskin jacket. The biggest job was sorting through the piles of his old books, but I enjoyed helping him because there was so much good stuff. I'd sit in his big fluffy armchair with a mug of chai, surrounded by mountains of books of all shapes and sizes, feeling like a kid in a candy shop.

One afternoon when we were almost finished sorting it all out, I found a copy of a David Attenborough book called *The Blue Planet* buried at the bottom of a drawer. I leafed through it, savouring the amazing pictures, and I came to this gorgeous image of a dolphin just like our one. I wanted to show Steve, so I held the page open for him.

"Look at that!" I said, grinning as I passed the book over towards him. He stared a moment at the photo, hesitant to hold the book in his hand. Then he took it in his fingers gingerly, like you'd hold a tarantula, and his face was frozen with shock.

He started talking then, but he looked across me without seeing me, his gaze focused on some distant object.

"Niamh bought it for me," he said softly. "After we'd watched the series together. We'd curl up on the sofa on Wednesdays ... "

He flipped the pages back, read the note that she'd written in the front, and suddenly he crumpled against me sobbing, a great storm passing through him. I rubbed his back and held him, saying the same words over and over.

"It's alright. Everything's alright."

IN MEMORIAM

Roshanara Voetzsch

For a short moment it is as if I can hear you breathing behind me. In the twilight state between dreaming and waking my mind plays tricks on me and everything seems to be all right for this very short moment. Sometimes I can even feel the mattress giving way under me as it used to when you joined me in bed.

This is why, since you left, I haven't been able to share my bedroom with anyone: I don't want to share the precious few moments I have with you. Somehow I still think you watch over me while I'm sleeping. Maybe sharing something as private as sleeping with anyone but you is a betrayal; maybe I will never be able to learn to trust someone as I trusted you.

I close my eyes, unwilling to regain full consciousness. I treasure those rare moments we share before the day breaks. It is as if I could sense your warmth, and it makes me feel safe again. In my mind your features are unchanged as I see you lying next to me, your greenish ginger-coloured eyes closed as you breathe evenly. I lie on my side and open my own, but the image of you doesn't fade.

When I finally turn on my back again I only see the white of the ceiling and your face fades in my memory. I desperately try to hang on to those images of us. The day we walked in the Bois de Boulogne with your dog dragging you through the park. One cold winter evening when we played cards all night because we both were too broke to afford a night out. A day up in the North of France having a picnic with your brother and sister, sitting in the field, drinking red wine and eating bread and cheese. As I lie here, more memories begin to haunt me. Our wedding day for example, the most important day in my life.

It was a small ceremony with only your brother and sister present. I recall a surge of happiness and a sudden sense of freedom when you put the wedding band on my finger. I had finally come home. For the first time in my life I felt at peace and complete. Everything made sense and nothing could take me away from you. I never stopped loving you and I'm sure I never will. Love is something that binds you beyond death, as my father once said: "No one is ever forgotten as long there is someone who remembers."

I catch a glimpse of my left hand, which is resting on my stomach, I lift it up and the light is reflecting on my wedding ring. They all told me that the pain will fade with time: it didn't.

Before tears threaten to overwhelm me, I move my hand to where I think my heart is and listen to its beat for a little while. It calms me down. You told me that it helped you to focus again when things became too much as was often the case. For me it was different - just lying on your chest and hearing your heartbeat took all my anxieties away. With your arm around me you assured me that everything would be fine and I should stop worrying. Often you would turn slightly, kiss me and then wait until I fell asleep.

Back then I could fall asleep in someone's arms. I can't anymore. Now I have to listen to my own heartbeat because yours has stopped beating forever.

Once we stood in a church and promised to love each other forever. "No," I hear you saying, "until death parts us!"

Surviving you was the hardest thing I had to do in my whole life.

UNDRESSING FRANCESCA

ADRIENNE ANIFANT

He was the only person wearing a full suit on a Saturday morning in Central Park. That's how I knew it was Sal. Or maybe it was the way I felt warm when I recognised the familiar movements of his body; the way he tilted forward watching the fast pace of his own feet. The scrappy Shih Tzu scrambled behind, whimpering for him to slow down. I never liked the dog but loved the collar. The fact that Sal put a spiked, leather collar on his purebred Shih Tzu was reason enough for me to date him. The man had a sense of humour. I could even get over the suit.

He squinted in the sun as he turned to talk to the struggling pup, and then stopped to let him have a rest. His eyes interrogated the park's expanse, searching for an end to his unwinding spool of thoughts. When his head slowly returned to my bench I looked away, pretending I wasn't there. Originality was never my strength.

The lake seemed cool and still in the autumn dawn. The swans glided with regal arrogance, nipping each other in the behind to clear their course. Ruthless creatures, swans were. I remember reading once where a swan broke a dog's neck, and held the slack body under water in efforts to protect her wounded mate. Sal was walking towards me, could feel it; the rhythm of his gait. I continued to find intrigue with the small lake reflecting the upper west side. The brush of grass underneath his sweeping stride sounded lush. The clinking change in his loose pockets was familiar and good.

"Frankie?"

I inspected a potential hole in my stocking, I wanted him to say my full name.

"Aey. Francesca," he shouted, stretching the vowels like a true Brooklyn native. He pinched his fingers like a bud and shook them in the air to emphasise his angst.

"Turn up the hearing aid, baby cakes." He had the charm of a stingray, but I fell for him every time. My eyes followed the perfectly creased seams of his pants. The Greek brow hung heavy over brown eyes that were prisms of happy and sad. A scar was under his left eye, to which he brought his hand immediately, as if he could hear my thoughts. His waist was leaner and cheeks hollow, I felt a moment of hope that maybe my absence was the cause. Nice try.

"Hi Sal, you're standing on my foot." I wrestled my foot from under his size fourteens and made him room, hoping he'd stay and hoping he'd leave.

"Yah, well I just want ya to know I'm here." He shifted his tie from side to side and forced a cough.

"Are you alone, sister or do ya want to be alone or what?" Sal raked his fingers through his black hair watching Park Avenue through the trees. I knew this was difficult for him, actually surprised he made the effort to come over.

"Yah, you can sit, but keep the dog on the other side."

"Frank, you were just jealous cause you knew Sappho was my real baby." He gave my thigh a familiar slap and shoved me over.

Sal fumbled in his pocket for his cell phone as I bit my nail. I'd come to despise the little Sony 2002 Elf that he'd bought at his family's electronic store on Lexington and 51st from his uncle of all people. I could smell the age of cell phones coming like I could smell the Reagan years, and for me they were equally as painful. I told Sal we should just wait for surgically implanted chips, complete multi-media Internet access from the stem of our brains.

"I need it for the business, doll-face." I hated it when he pretended we were in the forties and that "his business" was an underground cell of the New York drug trade for which he needed to be accessible at all times. Sal owned an authentic Gyro deli in the middle of SoHo. The messiest thing that ever happened there was during a phase when Sal wanted to rediscover his Grecian roots. After asking a woman if she came with fries, she threw a tub of organic yoghurt in his face, letting the door click gently behind her.

"But Sal, think how those incessant rings are training our brains to respond like dogs."

"I need to keep tabs on José, hopefully that sweet-assed Mexican will burn my shithole to the ground."

The phone moved in on a Saturday and it was already sleeping beside the bed on Sunday night. It wasn't so bad. I grew to like waking up to the sandpapery electric alarm of Senesino, Casanino, and Farinelli. Somehow Sal downloaded a ring from his favourite, Alessandro Moreschi, the last castrato opera singer in Italy. He had a few loves of his life and castrato singers were one of them. But I began to worry when Alessandro started singing regularly at 3:00am.

"Who was that?" I'd murmur, my back to Sal.

"José. He was just closing up." Liar, I thought.

The leaves now lapped the tumbling wind as we sat in the quiet park. The space between our arms was like a vortex. Sal nudged Sappho with his toe. He turned the phone off and I felt his fingers touch my blouse.

"What are you doing?" I pushed him away.

"Damn baby, this little guy was just crawlin' on your shirt. I know you hate them." He let the spider run along his fingers and into his palm. He let him go on the bench, watching the insect frantically scrub itself clean.

"Are you still leaving?" I took my ring off and rolled it between my fingers. His answer was low with shame.

"Three weeks, Joey will take over the business." Sal put a piece of gum in his mouth and rested his elbows on his knees.

"The West isn't that great. It's still riding on the coat tails of the Cowboy decade. East coasters just need the myth." My ring fell in the grass and Sal picked it up and twirled it on his finger.

"We've got a shitload of myths here sugarlump, but ya know I appreciate your cynicism." He was getting ready to leave; my stomach fell ten stories. He cupped his thick hand around my knee and touched my hand.

"Your ass is getting bigger but I'd still put you between two slices of bread." He laughed then tilted his head to manoeuvre a kiss on my neck. Bastard. Neck-kisses were the worst.

"I'll call ya."

"Who are you going with Sal?" I yelled after him, feeling splinters of reprove from the old park bench. It had seen this all before — broken hearts with no shame and nothing more to lose.

"No one baby. I just need to get outta here and have myself a think," he said without turning around. A red leaf crumbled under my shoe as I twisted it into the grass. I thought of the letters from José, tattered and worn from several readings, hidden under the mattress. I remembered the weekly, then monthly, lapses between sex, wondering if I was losing my touch. He laughed when he found my various sex-guides that I had begun to collect in hopes that some trick or turn would bring his roaming hands back to my body. I thought of the evenings reserved for José's English lessons, which only made me laugh. It was a miracle that anything out of Sal's mouth was deemed English. I thought of that fucking phone ringing several times during the night. And Sal running to the bathroom, talking low. Nervous and excited. The standard brew for new love. Sal was never the best at disguise. I needed to find a funeral.

I breathed in and imagined the oxygen molecules crystallizing in each ventricle of my lungs. The air was moist with the memory of rain and smelled briny and new, like a menstruating woman.

Outside the church, I gathered my hair into a clip, smoothing down unruly strands with my fingertips. I wanted to be inconspicuous and move like a shadow among the mourning bodies, bent and twisted in prayer. I slipped through the oak doorframe into the stone structure. The cool smell of stone and incense always made me feel my mortality.

The blackness of the coffin that lay before the altar absorbed the one, small stream of dusty light. The chapel rumbled with low voices and hushed whispers; frosty-haired women rested their heads against one another and held shrivelled hands, exchanging sobs like secrets. Behind them, little girls locked and unlocked their knees pretending the pew was a balance beam while their eyes danced on the arc of youth. The priest was talking to one of the old women in the front; his back was concave and he held her pale face between his hands as if he were looking into the eyes of a pup. His azure robes rippled around his body like small waves, rising and falling with the ebb of his movements. He was young with chiselled American features and looked more like he played for the Yankees than the Lord.

I sat in the back and watched the chalice on the altar break the candlelight. Sal and I went to a stranger's funeral every month. It was originally Sal's idea and when he mentioned it to me the first time, naked and propping his head off the pillow, I thought I had just slept with Charles Manson.

"It's good for the chakra, karma, or whatever. Ya know, to tip your hat to some random fart, so it ain't just some guy anymore."

I thought he was sick and I the sicker for letting him use my toothbrush and wear my robe but I went along. I can't say I felt like doing cartwheels afterwards but I *did* feel more alive. My sister accused us of using someone's death to freshen our own mortality. Maybe, but we paid attention to the words spoken about each person, when the words were the only things remaining. I started to write down their names and the things that their relatives or friends said in the elegies; the stories that echoed throughout each church hall. Sal would cock his head to the left and squint his eyes in concentration.

"Make sure you remember that baby, make sure you write it down."

Work was always a means to curb my personal life, so I walked to the office after the funeral feeling half dead, watching the mud stains on my Nine West boots. Saturday morning unravelled with the predictability and routine that was once pleasant, now insufferable. The directionless, sweet wandering of Saturday that you share with someone who enjoys the unique way you drift now seemed cruel; cruel to magnify, enhance my loneliness. The streets, cafes and vegetable markets were foreign now and the anonymity which cities either grant or curse was a godsend. People's diminished physicality, their increasing transience, allowed me to find a corner in the hive and hide.

I counted the number of tangled condoms and their various colours that led me to my office door. 42nd and Broadway was New York's catwalk for prostitutes. I remembered every time Sal and I were in a fight I'd go to work early in order to escape the silence of our bed. I'd usually catch some of the women working overtime, catching the early-bird CEO workaholics. Tapping their heels with impatience, they'd chuckle with one another, probably over another sloppy client.

"Morning Jezebel, Mary." (After mother, not Magdalene.) "Doing overtime on a Saturday?" I fought with my key chain.

"That's the only thing you can't do, hon. It does you. These fuckers are startin' to work on Saturday. We're thinkin' of leadin' the reform campaign for governmental restrictions on working hours.

"What are you, the fuckin' guardsman for the Louvre?" They eyed my bundle of keys with mirth, nudged one another with scabby elbows and kicked a can at my shoe. I pushed the door in with my hip. "See you, girls."

"Hey Frank, don't worry, he'll apologise by noon." My body cramped at their reference as I closed the oak door. Jezebel was a mother of two and looked the part. Mary was covered in tattoos and wore jeans, a T-shirt and work boots. She could give a shit. I liked her style.

The morning sun flirted with daylight as I threw my briefcase on the couch. The snoozing office, bereft of telephone rings, failing copiers, and astringent light from Edison's warm light bulb on Prozac, was quite archaic.

Our press published mostly cookbooks with authors as diverse and flavourful as their food. The Fords, authors of *The Barbecue Bible*, always showed up for meetings wearing their aprons and had that simple southern way of speaking, freckled with enough y'alls and goshes to send any New Yorker off their narrow precipice of sanity. The author of *The All-American Vegetarian Cookbook* had a penchant for horror movies with maximum carnage and the *Country Breadbasket* scribe was known for working himself into every oven he could open. The author of *Joys of Middle-Eastern Cooking* submitted his manuscript with a self-designed cover of George Bush and Saddam Hussein setting fire to a baked Alaska. I was the only one impressed.

I walked to the white landscape of paper and pen caps under which my desk hid. The press's collection of books resisted shelf life, preferring to lay with the third of Alaska's forests, flattened and compressed to the jungle of fax messages and author's complaints that crept and crawled across the expanse of my cubicle.

The walls of Beacon Hill Press enfolded the whispers of women taunted by the sexy youthfulness of capitalism; warehouse walls with heavy industrial brick and sweeping windows through which workers once watched a city brimming with notions of itself in the early nineteenth century. Ray Stewart, the head patron and god-like publisher, sardonically told me the first day I began work that this warehouse was where some of the first women worked for paid labour. In a corner by the stereotypical water-cooler hung a black and white photo of the women; four rows of straight backs and high chins, the pride and excitement still emanating from their grainy, unfocused faces. What were their thoughts? Did they envision great things, new beginnings, futures as bright as city lights against the night? They worked steadily for twelve hours, interrupted for only a half-hour lunch, sewing linen and suckling what would become an infamous work ethic in its infancy.

I liked to put my palm on the pocked wooden floor when I was alone, trying to feel the vibration of their anxious heels and silent screams. All three hundred and fifty-seven women were burnt alive when one of the machines caught on fire. The doors were all locked and windows too thick to break; the women burned beneath their sewing machines, crying out to a vain, taciturn city. I said a mental good morning and looked out.

"I miss Sal," I told the brick wall outside my window, as it absorbed the first tears of morning sun. *Why,* it asked.

"Fuck off," I said.

Police sirens and ambulance wails became louder and more frequent. All part of a city's morning yawn and stretch. I looked at my wrist for the watch that was never there, and decided it was time to work. I had to photograph the food and have a cover design for a cookbook in the mail by 5.00pm. Its title was *Grandma Boreman's 350 favourite ways to celebrate Thanksgiving*. The best part was that the author was Joe Boreman, the man who made millions from morphing the grilled cheese sandwich into a portable delicacy. Not only had Boreman not spoken to his grandmother in ten years, but he had compiled his repertoire of recipes from the backs of soup can labels. Boreman was walking the fine line on plagiarism, but Ray still saw dollar signs.

Trying to excavate my desk for a tube of glue was like searching for pieces of pottery or fragments of mammoth bone in Death Valley. Nothing was surfacing. The glue was used to make food shine and to defy those stubborn principles of gravity and time. I threw aside some packages of Styrofoam which I used to stuff desserts with, making them voluptuous.

"Make 'em pout, sex sells." That was Ray's advice when I began photographing food for covers rather than sending projects out of house. He sat across from me, legs wide open and hands clasped behind his head. I blinked at his toothy smile, with pen erect and pages of blank paper. It never ceased to baffle me. Did his genius lie in deliberate reservation, in simple statements that were like spires around which I had to build the church? Did he write haikus and understand the muscle behind their heft? Had he read Confucius? Most likely not, but he had read psychological profiles of the graduates of all-women colleges. Work hungry, self conscious, approval-seeking predators. Those were my sisters.

Be spare with your instructions and expectations and we will overshoot them by miles just to cover ourselves. Whatever the reason, women college graduates are freebasing on success and superiority within the spheres of money, law reform, or home making and we'll fuck whoever we must to achieve it, literally. Bruce understood this and played us like Coltrane on the sax, manning his office of eight with five alumnae from Smith, Wellesley, and Barnard, fully locked and loaded.

The glue was stuck to a proposal for a Polish-American cookbook that I had yet to approve. It made a return landing to the battlefield, strewn with envelope carcasses and office supplies. Careful not to trip on the newly laid Mexican throw rugs, I headed for the photography studio.

Black velvet cloaks were thrown over the cameras in the windowless room. They looked like a gothic nightmare; headless horsemen balancing on three skeletal legs. For a moment, I knew them as sinister intruders in all their contours of blackness. Marked huntsmen who'd commit less harm if they would shoot to kill. Rather, their lenses promised immortality, permanence, and salvation from this flawed flesh.

The fluorescent lights blinked, filling the room with a synthetic hum. I removed the fabric to reveal their lifeless steel. The roasted chicken I prepared yesterday was on the counter, encircled with cherry tomatoes. After researching photographers' secrets on the web and scouring the library, I invented my own anti-ageing remedy for food. I called it wrinkle cream, made from motor oil, Windex and a fetching combination of other happy household poisons. It worked best with meats but also gave vegetables that shower fresh glow. While injecting it into the turkey with a medical syringe and basting its tawny skin, I thought of Sal. The evening I told him about the first chicken injected with my resourceful, cost-efficient wrinkle cream, he was lying on the couch with cucumber slices over his eyes.

"Jesus bunny baby, that poor motherfucker was executed twice! And the second time was more humane, that's the weird fuckin' thing. Give him a break."

I looked, now, at the Thanksgiving turkey pumped with so many chemicals it could be declared an environmental hazard, and squirted more toilet cleaner and hairspray on its legs, so they appeared lean and sleek. Placing the cyborg turkey on the table along with an apple pie and a woven basket filled with stalks of corn, I remembered how on Friday, Bruce had said:

"Needs more bust." I looked down. He gave me an *I'm-not-a-scumbag-but-I'll-laugh-anyways* laugh.

"No, you're fine. The pie, the pie! It needs depth, it needs bosoms!" Bastard. I removed the shrivelling apples and stuffed the pie with Styrofoam.

The low-hanging lamplight flooded the table like an altar or a poker table. Either way, the stakes were high. I adjusted the camera lens and zoomed in on the culinary ensemble. *I'm ready for my close-up, Mr DeMille*. It was incredible, the turkey and pie looked like a sweet and savoury masterpiece, yet they had enough toxins and chemicals to kill a small country. I couldn't smell them, couldn't even touch them unless I wanted the pads of my fingertips to sizzle.

The camera shutter snapped like a nine millimetre pistol, and I said a prayer to my girls soaked in the floorboards, that Ray would be happy with the synthetic implants.

CLOUD NINE

I should have remembered, no need to
even check; nine is always full, always.

And they never pick up the phone. Six
or seven can be accessed easily enough

if you time it right. Sometimes even eight.
Skip to ten and you're over the top.

Yes, nine is the tricky one. Occasionally you
meet people who say they have been there,

but it's hard to tell. I mean, if true what
are they doing out here with the rest of us?

GERARD HANBERRY

ROCKY DEVALERA

Stephen Shields

"There's no doubt it's a fine building," said DeValera to his Minister for Foreign Affairs, Frank Aiken. "It rather dwarfs our Leinster House, Frank, or do they call you Mr Aiken around here, heh! heh!"

They were walking across the plaza to the United Nations building in New York. The year was 1957.

Meanwhile, at the maintenance bay to the same building, a decrepit van with the legend *Frankenstein and Son, Electricians – Microwave Ovens a Specialty* came to a halt. Two men got out of the van. One had grey hair and was obviously older than the other, but in every other particular they were identical. They had noses like parked JCBs with buckets folded and eyes that protruded like multiplying frogspawn. Each was named Dmitri Frankenstein.

"We take the elevator to the fourth floor and then to hospitality suite 13. The supervisor cannot be there, but he said to fit the cooker beside the fridge in the kitchenette," said the older man. "Dmitri, if this job works out just think how many microwave ovens we can fit in this building alone. The Frankenstein family fortunes will be restored. Perhaps in a few years we will be able to buy back Castle Frankenstein in Transylvania."

"I don't like these new microwaves, Pop. They're too complicated for people to use. They'll never take off."

"Take off! Take off! Cook a dinner in five minutes. Then you can listen to the game, go to Radio City, go to the bar. People will love them," countered the elder.

"But look at the size. It's bigger than any cooker I've ever seen."

"Ah, problems! Problems! Always problems with you, Dmitri."

DeValera and Aiken waited in the foyer of the building for the Irish ambassador. At 12.05pm DeValera was tapping his wristwatch. "Five minutes late already."

Dmitri the son balanced the gigantic load delicately on his trolley and backed towards the service lift. As he stepped over the threshold, his heel caught and he lurched sideways with his load. He managed to stabilise both himself and the microwave before everything could hit the ground.

"You crummy hick," said the elder. "Now look what you've done."

"But, Pop, it didn't fall."

"'But Pop' … such palaver. Look at that button panel on the elevator."

The panel was hanging by a mesh of green and white wires, where the corner of the microwave had hit it. There was a slow sizzle from the panel, then silence. The lift mechanism swooned and stopped too. Dmitri junior jabbed at the button marked four. The lights in the lift flickered, then the two Frankensteins were in total darkness.

"You jerk," hissed the elder. "There could be a war if the elevators don't work in here. And who'll want a microwave oven in the middle of a war?"

"But Pop, there must be another elevator we can use. There are other shafts over there. Look!"

"My son may have had his bright idea for the day," pronounced the elder. "He thinks of another elevator. We'll try it if it pleases the Boy Genius."

They managed to get the microwave back on the trolley and reversed into the new lift.

"Now Pop," said the younger, "How do we reach the button?"

But before his father could answer this question, the doors on the lift closed and it began to rise.

"Now you load us in like sardines," said the elder . "How on my grandfather's grave do we get out? Huh! Genius Boy!"

The lift came to a halt and the doors opened.

"Is there anyone there?" asked the elder.

"Yes," came the rather startled voice of a woman.

"What floor is this?"

"The fourth."

"Good. Would you mind standing back, we have to deliver this machine on this floor."

"We'll never get out. Not with this machine," groaned Junior.

"Panic, always panic. Here's how we do it. Just put your back to the machine and push."

And so they did, their legs against the back wall. A screeching noise was heard and then with a final pop the machine tumbled onto its front and the two Dmitris shot through the air. They landed at the feet of the woman waiting to use the lift. She looked at them, hesitated for a moment and then retreated up the corridor.

"Now look what you've done."

"Is that any way to speak to your father?"

Then they noticed another panel with green and white wires dangling from the lift, heard the familiar soft sizzle and the silence afterwards.

It was 12.45pm and DeValera was upset. Lack of punctuality led to bad negotiations he thought. At last the Irish Ambassador emerged from the door to a stairwell and raced towards them.

"I'm awfully sorry about the time. Some silly buggers have messed up the whole lift system and the building is in chaos."

"Unparliamentary language, however provoked, does not become a member of the Diplomatic Corps," came DeValera's comment.

"We'll have to go up by the stairs. At least it's only the fourth floor. I had to come from our offices on the seventeenth."

As this was going on, a massive man smiling hugely entered the main concourse. He was accompanied by an entourage of about twenty people. As they passed in, the big man stood back and held the door open for a group of Asians leaving the building.

"So dis is de United Nations," he said. "Does anyone here speak English? Ha! Ha! Dat's a joke, Coach."

"Yeah Champ!" said a man with a clean sweep of baldness from his eyebrows to the poll of his head bounded by two tramlines of brilliantined hair on either side. Below his eyes his face crumpled into folds.

"All we have to do is talk to dis lady at the desk and she'll get Giuseppe for us. Right!"

The receptionist picked up an internal phone.

"The Italian ambassador will meet you at Suite 14, fourth floor," she said. "It may take him a little time. He's coming from the seventeenth floor and there's something wrong with the elevators, but he's on his way already."

On the fourth floor, the Frankensteins had managed to get the machine upright and move it along to Suite 13. They looked at the door. They looked at the machine. They looked at each other.

"I don't know that it'll fit, Pop," said Dmitri the younger.

"Pessimism! Pessimism! Always the worst," said his father.

"It could be broken, Pop. From the fall and that."

"Pessimism! If I had a hat I'd dance on it," spat the elder, making a few token movements with his feet on an imaginary hat.

"Maybe Pop, we could bring the plug back through the door to a socket inside and make sure it's working. Before we have to haul it through that door."

"Sometimes, son, I can see the Frankenstein blood flow through your veins." Dmitri the elder took the plug and made his way into Suite 13. "Son, you will have to move the microwave oven closer. The cable's not long enough."

"Okay Pop! I'll just pull it in a little closer here now." This was followed by a grunt. "How's that?"

"No, you'll have to pull it in around the corner a little."

"Oh! Oh! Pop. I think I pulled it too far and I've jammed it in the doorway."

"I should have known better. Why can nothing go right when you're involved. Still I suppose we better make the best of it. I'm plugging it in."

Silence from the machine.

DeValera counted the Hospitality Suites along the corridor: 10, 11, 12, followed by a long gap where that peculiar machine stood, then 14. Room 13 was missing.

"Superstition in the UN," he observed drily.

"Or a new ambassador to the UN," thought the ambassador. Would nothing go right?

They stood in the hallway, unsure for a moment. A huge man ambled towards them followed by a large entourage.

"Could you tell me where Suite 14 is?"

"I believe it's just there," said DeValera pointing up the corridor. "It's only our Room 13 that seems to have disappeared."

"Huh! You've lost your room, dat's tough luck. We'd share ours, wouldn't we boys? If it didn't belong to da UN."

Just then a small sleek man appeared.

"Here's our man now. Dis is Giuseppe. Our man."

"I know Giuseppe, Signor Agnelli, well. He is the Italian ambassador here. Our rooms are close together on the seventeenth Floor. They're alphabetically aligned, you see. This is our Taoiseach, Mr DeValera."

"And this is Rocky Marciano, an Italian American, of whom we're proud," said Giuseppe, "the World Champion."

"Da undefeated Heavyweight Champion," insisted Rocky. "Tee-Shock. Dat's an interestin' name. Is it Irish?"

"No it means he's the Prime Minister in our country," explained the ambassador.

"Sort of like da President? We have a president. Hey coach, what's da name of our president?"

"Eisenhower, Champ."

"Yeah. Eisenhower. We met him. He's a good president, a good guy."

"I believe our room may be hidden behind that electrical machine," said DeValera.

"Dat's unfortunate," said the Champ. "Can I help?"

He stepped towards the machine to pull it away, but only caught the door, which sprang open.

"Has this something to do with your television?" asked DeValera.

"No, dat's no television," said the Champ. "What are these sort of nozzle things hanging out of it?"

"I rather think they look like skullcaps," said DeValera.

"Dey look like showers for midgets to me. Hey dey fit on your head," said the Champ. "Hey Tee-Shock — try this."

"When in Rome do as the Romans do," laughed DeValera, and he placed the other skullcap on his head.

Inside Room 13, the Frankensteins were intent on making the machine work.

"Hey, Pop," said the younger, throwing two switches.

There was a brief hum and a flash of tubes and bulbs but then again silence.

"Let me see," said the exasperated elder. "But this is no microwave oven, Dmitri. I haven't seen a machine like this for years. This is grandfather's machine. I ask you to bring out a microwave oven from the store, and look what you do. This is the old transference machine Grandpa had to hide when he fled, I mean left, Transylvania."

"Did you feel a tingle?" asked DeValera.

"Sure did," said the Champ. "Like stickin' your finger in the light socket. Hey, Tee-Shock, you got stains on your forehead."

"Funny. I was going to say the same thing to you Mr Marciano," said DeValera, wiping his temples.

"Nope," said the Champ. "They're still there. You'll need a scrubbin' with soap and water. Here, I'll move da machine outta da way."

He lifted it cleanly out of the doorway. The Frankensteins were exposed staring into the space, Dmitri the younger holding a red cord.

The meeting was over and DeValera was being driven uptown. "Could we drive by Madison Square Garden?" he asked, "and soak up the atmosphere? You know, the smell of the canvas and the thought of that seething crowd and the urgency of the bell … "

"Hey, you got the ring of a real champ about you Mr DeValera," laughed the chauffeur.

Two weeks later Frank Aiken and Sean Lemass were in the Taoiseach's office. Lemass was seated in front of the Taoiseach's desk while Aiken stood behind him. DeValera was near the window, skipping.

"We've got to be careful on this one, Chief. MacBride's a canny operator and I'm not sure that our man is being totally upfront with us. That Locke's Distillery business is dangerous. One slip and there might be no recovery," said Lemass. "A right bloody mess."

"Yes," concurred Aiken. "MacBride's got hold of some information. I'd love to know his source and we might be able to put a halt to his gallop."

"251, 252, 253, 254 … " went DeValera, hardly breaking sweat. "I'm nearly there, Coach."

The Champ was sitting on the fire escape outside Coach's Apartment.

"What ya doin' Champ?"

"I'm lookin' at da comely maidens down by da basketball."

"Huh Champ!"

"Da comely maidens. Dey'll be dancin' soon in da twilight. And hey, dose fellas shouldn't be black. Dey should be white wid deir woollen vests tucked into their underpants and wielden' deir hurlin' sticks wid skill and athleticism … Hey Coach."

"Yeah Champ."

"What's a sliotar?"

"I'm worried, very worried," said Frank Aiken to Lemass in Lemass's office. "The Chief doesn't seem to be taking this thing seriously at all. He's obsessed with this fitness lark. He was lying on the floor of his office when I went there last night and he had a volume of the *Encyclopaedia Brittanica* in each hand. He was raising them up and down in rapid motion. He asked me to time him. Said he was trying to get up to twenty a minute. The *Encyclopaedia Brittanica*. He hasn't touched anything British since 1916."

"Still he's always had the safest pair of hands in the business," said Lemass, "though I'd never noticed how big they were until recently. They'd remind you of a heavyweight."

The Champ was winding down after his day's training in the gym.

"Hey Coach," he said, "whaddya think of da special position of the Catholic Church? Ya know, freedom of religion and worship for everyone but special for da Catholic Church 'cause there's so many of dem."

"Yeah Champ, whadever you say."

"Yeah … and dere's da question of da mother in da home. Now dat's a theme dat's close to my heart."

Coach was worried. Where was Champ getting all these kooky ideas? He must have been talking to a Jesuit.

Lemass and Aiken flanked DeValera on his way to the Dáil Chamber and Taoiseach's Question Time. DeValera moved fluidly between them with a certain menace.

Sean MacBride rose to speak.

"Would the Taoiseach like to condemn the appalling situation at Locke's Distillery where hundreds of ordinary people, and taxpayers, have lost thousands of pounds due to the sinister manoeuvrings of businessmen and I am sorry to say public figures?"

"You won't trap me in the corner," said DeValera, feinting and spinning one way and then the other. "Bob and weave, bob and weave," he whispered.

Lemass sank further into his seat.

A clamour arose in the opposition benches.

"You're avoiding the issue ..."

"Face the facts ... "

"You can't take it on the chin!"

The Ceann Comhairle's bell rang out, "Order! Order!"

"End of round one," said DeValera. "Back to the corner." He dived out of the Dáil Chamber and headed for his office.

Back in the Taoiseach's den, an exasperated Lemass said, "Chief, you've got to get back out there and deal with this issue. Go on the attack. It's the only way."

DeValera was shadowboxing before a portrait of Earnan de Blaghad.

"Gee, this fellow must have taken a terrible mauling in the ring," said DeValera. "Just look at his face. That nose has been smashed and his whole face is a pulp."

"Yes," said Aiken, "I agree with Sean. We should go on the attack."

"Yes," said DeValera. "Hit and move! Hit and move!"

"God, Chief! We've got to take this thing seriously. MacBride is at the top of his form and he's a hard hitter."

"Yes," said DeValera, "he's a hard hitter alright, but can he go the full fifteen rounds?"

INTRODUCTION TO WOODS

Burnt Church, New Brunswick

I want you to feel the wildness
of a Canadian forest
that frightened your father.
The fear of getting lost,
the fear of feral animals and of trees.
No trees in Connemara,
not like these!
Dry twigs snap underfoot
overgrown paths scratch,
branches whip back as you walk quietly
listening to the forest.

We make our way
to the turbulent brook,
careful, once there, to hold onto something
as we lower our foot into icy water to be tickled,
massage by quicksand.

On the way back,
a stop to eat berries
and examine moose tracks in the dirt
while mosquitoes get high on untainted blood.
They take out chunks of flesh
with an itch to drive you demented.

Later to take refuge on a sea breeze
out of the enclosure
and on to the waves of the Atlantic,
yes, the same Atlantic,
rocking as the wind picks up to a storm.
Waves break high on the boat deck
As they do over the promenade in Salthill.

Then, motor not responding,
we are stranded out at sea,
rain comes down in sheets onto your slim
bathing-suited forms, while an uncle
gives you rum for warmth. Ride it out
until a tug is sent to the rescue.

I watch the wildness take hold,
you catch the power of the untamed.

SANDE BUNTING

SLEEPLESS

When you are sleeping with the dragon
there is little alternative but to float on its breath.

I close my eyes to hear a dance of crows,
a racket of quick Morse code on a tin roof.

Rain on the skylight
is the click of my dog's paws on a wooden floor.

In sleep I drift along the canal,
blue umbrellas float beneath the surface
raindrops make tiny circles, a fish jumps.

In a clump of reeds a coot weaves in,
the heron is hard to spot,
elegant with neck stretched,
the transformation to an old man
nothing more than a shrug.

Morning's so ordinary.

SANDRA BUNTING

HALIFAX, NOVA SCOTIA

For my father WRC Bunting

My child, your granddaughter,
rolled in a pile of crumpled leaves
in the middle of the park
tossing vibrant reds, golds and oranges
up into the salty air at noon.
A clock from the citadel
set off seagulls screeching a lament.
The air turned.
Autumn nipped lazy sunshine
Colours faded around the edges.
On the harbour the foghorn
piped out a military air.
At your bed I tried to keep you,
not letting you free to blend with the sky.
But for a minute my attention wavered.
I turned and you were gone.

SANDRA BUNTING

MOTHER FROM OUTER SPACE

I thought you an alien.
Barefooted and flannelette night-gowned,
I crept into your bedroom in the middle of the night,
past an ashtray of stale cigarette butts
and a foul-smelling amber potion to see
your face as you communicated with the stars.

Fully clothed, eyes shut, on your back
you spoke your own language.
I would listen to each utterance to break the code
to learn the secrets of the Universe
until you turned over onto your side,
and erupted in snores.

On rainy days when you were busy,
I went through your drawers meticulously
and found, under beaded cocktail purses,
lacy black gloves, the glittery stole from Paris,
an old newspaper with an article about UFOs.

SANDRA BUNTING

EXILE

A stone stands alone like a little man
and I stand alone from a land of snow,
between tall trees and icy sea.
My home is among rocks now
rain pellets beat time on glass
as morning sun tries to come out.
A dancer in the window moves
parts of her body in isolation.
A donkey brays over a convent wall,
a call to look at daffodils outside
and the stone in the lessening rain
by a little hand keeping me here.

SANDRA BUNTING

A WASH OF PALE SKY

HELENA MULKERNS

There are bars on the window. He sits ragged in the dusk, turning a piece of processed cheese over and over on the cracked plate. It's his dinner, actually. One slice of cheese and one piece of sliced pan. Stale - who will notice? Not them, apparently. And if they get the heel of the bread, tough buns. He is silhouetted against the bars of the dining room window, quiet.

"Hi, Lisa," he says, barely looking up. "How's it going?"

Behind him, a moss-coloured line of wet is creeping down the tiles. The smell is old country convent, dank as a morgue, riddled with mould. The linoleum is grimy; the walls are painted green above the grubby white chest-high tiling. Why would they do that, now, paint the walls horrible green, shiny? But it matches the clunky pre-war furniture, the peeled-edge Formica table. The bulb overhead is bare, 40 watts max. It's a nightmare, but it's not hers. Almost worse that it's his.

The grim light deadens his beautiful, horrific cheekbones, transfixing her. She has come alone, in the damp and cold of this dead winter of 1973, defying strictest family orders. Now, she'd rather not hear what he is telling her, she would rather be lying with him on the lawn by the duck pond in Stephen's Green, in the June sunlight. Or in the noontide heat of the beach at Killiney, with afterwards the extravagance of under-age beers at the Dalkey Island Hotel. But she can't concentrate on this escape route, because he's being quite adamant.

"Ringo Starr stole my song, Lisa. That song in the charts right now, that he *says* he wrote, 'You're Sixteen' - you know it? I wrote that song, and Ringo stole it, man. I'm going to sue."

She considers laughing. But there is no telling how he would react. Crying does not have to be considered, it is just simmering under her confused smile. But not an option either, just now. She's afraid to hurt him, afraid to hear him. Afraid to be here — and at how the simple fragility of their world just collapsed down some psycho-mineshaft as she walked into this darkness. She is seventeen. She is beautiful. She is not his. She seeps love and pain and he turns over the slice of easy cheese once again.

The inmates bustle around. Some are in their own world, shuffling, whispering, tugging the front of their trousers shamefully, others are exhibitionistic. In the corner a woman is pulling her hair out, methodically. Seán takes no notice. He has important information to divulge.

"Last night, I went up the North, to the soldiers. They all had their own igloos. It was pretty isolated. Snowing, but they were warm in those army parkas. They were okay lads, you know?"

She nods, pictures Seán's imaginary soldiers in the snow, their rifles dark vertical lines against the fine white flakes descending, and does not know what to say. There are real men in prison up North these days, dragged in, kicking and screaming. They wouldn't say the soldiers were okay lads.

Seán was brought in here unconscious. He would hardly have offered resistance. Now he is conscious, but just about. They clearly have him controlled, despite his raving. She wonders what kind of drugs they are giving him, instead of his drugs of choice. Or is he really what they say? She doesn't even know what schizophrenic means. Psychotic tendencies exacerbated, perhaps irreversibly affected by non-prescribed use of mood-altering substances.

"There are rats, Lisa. They come when the attendants are not here."

"Yeah?"

"Lisa — " he leans forward. "Do you believe me? She looks at the filth in the corners of the room.

"Seán, I believe you." He nods, apparently satisfied.

"I think we should go to Bhutan, Lisa. That's where it's at right now. There's nothing bad there. Animals aren't afraid of people in the Himalayas, did you know that? The people are Buddhist, they believe in the equality of all that lives. Wild animals — mountain yaks, horses, goats — they'll walk right up to you, let you pet them. Because humans have never treated them badly, they've no reason to be afraid or defensive. That's true." Lisa hoped it was true.

"Okay, Seán, let's go to Bhutan, then. As soon as you're well."

"Promise?"

"Yeah, I promise."

"Please come and see me again."

"I promise."

In the summer of 1972 Seán's long, dark curls framed a face that was popularly thought to be a blend of Marc Bolan and Robert Plant. He wrote poetry, and he was very tall. The teachers in Blackrock College called him *gifted*. He was reading Rimbaud when the others were struggling through "Stony Grey Soil", and was fond of quoting (especially to those with no French), "*on n'est pas serieux quand on a dix-sept ans*" ...

And he wasn't, of course. He was rarely serious, except with Lisa, for a while. For eight months, he held her under a spell of wonder and light that defied all parental control. He painted flowers on her eyelids and took her to see Rory Gallagher in the National Stadium. They both shook Rory's hand as he leaned over the front of the stage, and she thought this was the best thing that happened all year. But it wasn't, Seán was.

In spring, they spent their afternoons burning incense in his bedroom, listening to *Tubular Bells*, *Dark Side of the Moon*, *Harvest* and *Ziggy Stardust*. He lived in a crumbling old house off Sydney Parade Avenue, with a straggly garden and twenty thousand books that lined the old corridors and rooms like wallpaper. He seemed older than his contemporaries.

He took her to an Ashram in Dun Laoghaire, where a bloke with a very long beard taught them meditation. They stayed a few times in a commune near the Glen of the Downs, run by an American called Chato. She used to get into terrible trouble at home for staying out, but later she would reflect that those mornings were the high point of her existence: waking up within quiet, whitewashed walls, dawn birdsong filling the ancient forest, with Seán's dark mane on the stripy, uncovered pillow.

But he was strange sometimes. Once, he accused her of stealing his shoes — they had a huge row. He was funny about where things were, and sometimes engaged in intricate, useless exercises like alphabetising his album collection. She had to admit he was definitely odd the day he freaked out when she put Cat Stephen's "Tea For the Tillerman" under "T", when of course, as he furiously informed her, it should have been under "S" for the artist's name. He would be serene, soft and captivating as a hovering dragonfly, but then turn on her fast, like a cornered animal — when there was no reason for it — and bite as vicious as a mink into her heart.

He went to London when she went back to finish high school, to the chagrin of his parents, who would have preferred to see him in Trinity. Waiting for the bus to go to school November mornings, she'd remember the sunny window seat in his room, them fitted into it like a jigsaw puzzle, with the lazy oak trees swaying in the garden outside.

In December, she was watching "Top of the Pops" in the front room, her brothers playing air guitar to Horslips' "Dearg Doom". The phone rang, and it was Sheila McCafferty asking her had she heard about Seán Herlihy, that he was back in a desperate state, and had to be hospitalised.

When Lisa went around to the house next day, Mrs Herlihy closed the front door in her face, so she walked over to visit Seán's granny, who just said he'd been "hauled off to Saint Brendan's like his great-uncle Peadar". Lisa looked at her blankly.

"*Grangegorman*, lovie" she whispered, in qualification. Grangegorman. The word was synonymous in Dublin with somewhere two stops up from hell itself. Lisa didn't even know why it scared her so much to hear the words, but when she eventually got there, it became very clear.

It was Saturday afternoon when she got on the bus in O'Connell Street, nervous because she was headed into the deep unknown of the city's Northside. The sheer dilapidation of the city all along the journey was depressing enough, but it was one of those grey, drizzle-days when even the most valiant soul feels the pall of mortality. She walked up by a stinky river to the entrance of the hospital, marked by huge, institutional gates. Going up the driveway, trying to reason with her brain on the wisdom of continuing up towards the spectre-ediface ahead, Granny Seán's words echoed in her head. "Lovie, it's not just the drugs, I have to tell you. He's been diagnosed, you see. Whatever he's been up to, it's brought it out of him — he's not well."

For a while, Seán haunted her, those moribund butterfly eyes flickering even into her dreams, *please come and see me again*. But despite her promise, Lisa didn't go back.

She did the Leaving, and she met Dave. That became the boring story of her life. Dave was clean and straightforward with a business sense that managed to combine his knowledge of football with a lucrative love for rock music. He'd never even heard of Rimbaud. Although she'd have been loath to admit it, Lisa was impressed by Dave's worldliness. His first record shop was in a basement off Grafton Street and before long had two more. He was the type that you rarely heard anyone badmouth, and he made her laugh. He gave Lisa her first job, after leaving school, and it wasn't hard to bridge the gap from employee to lover.

Lisa ran into Seán one more time, though, two years after the visit, at a party following some record launch. They had sex in a large, cold bathroom, with the noise of the revels outside crashing through the door, and The Stooges belting out "Fun House" on the loud speakers. Afterwards, back inside the fray of the party, they tried to talk. But the words flitted away from their wasted senses gravity-less, into the smoke-filled atmosphere, and somhow only sonic confusion filled Lisa's head.

Dave came across her later in the garden, crying, and chose that night to propose. Just as well, in a way. Seán was dead a month before she knew she was pregnant.

At the funeral, Dave was gentle and sympathetic, if a little surprised at her devastation. It was this big hearted kindness what she loved most about Dave, and that won her over to him, more than anything else.

After they were married, he got into promoting music, and a few years after Shane was born, when punk came rampaging in, he was well set up to give the garage bands a kick-start, in his new venue off King Street. All the while making a few bob for himself, of course. They moved to a comfortable, renovated cottage in Enniskerry. Then, when his record shops went national, he jumped on the home video bandwagon as well, and they moved to a sea view detached in Sandycove. It went on from there.

It was Christmas 1985, when Shane was nine, that Lisa found a small, sad, newspaper article in the Evening Herald, wrapped unwittingly around the base of the fresh pine Dave had brought home from Dunne's Stores. In the fairy lights, as her husband and son opened the boxes of decorations, her heart turned raw at the words on the page, "St. Brendan's Old Wing Condemned". It had been discovered, apparently, during a recent health-board survey, that inmates were suffering under "Victorian conditions". The Minister for Health closed it down with great fanfare, purporting to be outraged at the "inhumanity" suffered by his mentally challenged constituents. He razed the old wing to the ground, announcing that it should have been condemned after the First World War.

"What's wrong, Ma?" her boy whispered, and ran to the kitchen to get her a Kleenex. Dave just had that puzzled look on his face.

"Nothing pet," Lisa hugged Shane when he approached her with a tissue for her nose. "Mammy was just thinking of something that happened a long time ago. Nothing to worry about, really!"

Nothing to worry about for a long time, and then plenty. She began to worry about Shane somewhere between the point where the headmaster first phoned her at three o'clock in the afternoon wondering why her son wasn't in his biology class, to when he was caught stealing jeans in the new Southside shopping centre and hauled home by the local police. She and Dave couldn't figure out why Shane would ever need to steal things, they never left him short of money. He was a gentle kid, usually — this kind of carry on seemed so against his nature. But that was only the start of it.

Shane was beautiful. He charmed people generally, and he was able to wrap Lisa around his little finger, despite her attempts to be the dutiful mother. He would bring his guitar down to the kitchen and play to her — that was before he stopped writing songs. Before he started lying.

Dave was another matter. He and Shane couldn't be in the same room together for ten minutes without a row. Dave couldn't stand his endless theories: on life, science, literature. Literature my arse,he'd say. Why couldn't Shane work Saturdays in one of the record shops like a normal kid, learn the value of money? She never knew if Dave finally guessed the truth — you just had to look at the fine-boned, dark-eyed son, and then at the big, blond hulk of a man she married, to see it.

He began spending more and more time away, in the office or at gigs and music festivals, until he finally moved back to Enniskerry with a twenty year-old singer-songwriter from Nashville who'd discovered her Irish roots.

Shane was stoic — as he was becoming about everything, it seemed. He just grew more handsome, and more truculent. Always out. Or in the garage playing music, or else up in his room. In love with Björk and Kurt Cobain simultaneously, if you were to go by the posters. He was talking to Lisa less and less, except, increasingly, when he needed money. Then he would have exotic tales to justify his cash requirements. "Darragh O'Neill's mother's just had a car crash on the Bray road! I have to go and get Darragh – I need 20 quid taxi money!" It didn't occur to Lisa to question why a sixteen year old could precisely calculate that he needed 20 pounds for cab fare, she just gave it to him.

One Christmas Eve, Lisa ran into Shane in their local by accident, with his gang of friends. She went over to say hello, touched his shoulder, and as he turned around, she was assaulted by a neon shock wave of cop-on, so sharp she could hardly speak.

"Shane, hi …"

"Hey … "

The blue orbs, usually so soulful, were bleached and empty — tiny pin pupils in a wash of pale sky, expressionless. She had seen these eyes before, thought them chilling before she even knew what they meant. Now this, like a nightmare. Distracted, she backed off, smiling, dragging herself out to the car park, where she burst into tears. There was no denying the fact. She couldn't believe it, and yet she could. I mean, how could she have been so stupid … such a complete *idiot* …

She tried everything. Doctors, counsellors, whatever twelve-step programmes were there, even though she hadn't a clue what she was doing half the time. She would have done anything. Sometimes he played along, presumably to butter her up, but the worst thing was the lies. And the most unbelievable thing was how much she used to believe him — she wanted so much to believe him, and she could never get her head around the fact that her son was capable of such barefaced deception.

The first time he came home beaten up, the realisation hit her that he was one of those statistics they kept talking about in the papers, the scourge of the Dublin streets.

The afternoon she sat in the juvenile court for Shane's first charge, she felt like a creature from another planet amongst the other, tougher mothers and wives. The judge pronounced him a hard case, despite his youth. A hard case. Only by virtue of the boy's favourable background would he be lenient this once. She drove home with her drained, shaking child in the seat beside her. He asked her for money at one point on the way home, and they made a detour to an area she would ordinarily have avoided in daylight, let alone the encroaching dusk. When he got back in the car it was dark. He seemed relaxed, no longer shivering. She didn't need to ask why.

"Mrs Nolan?"

"Yes, Breda?" God, it was two o'clock in the morning. That girl who sometimes phoned for Shane.

"Mrs. Nolan ... " the voice broke down into messy sobs, "you have to go and get Shane ... " Lisa felt like somebody had punched her in the stomach, long distance.

"Where is he?"

"Down the back of Dorgan's car-park, in Lamb Street, near the old baths. He's very bad. They got him, they got him ... "

Lisa grabbed the car key, skidded out the drive, and broke red light after red light almost oblivious. As she turned left at the canal, she realized she'd no idea what she was going to find.

When she finally got to Lamb Street, there was nothing to indicate anybody was there in the dark, empty car park of Dorgan's furniture warehouse. Breda had promised to phone for an ambulance, but the street was empty. She opened the car door, and a shaft of light shot out across the darkness. Then, there in the middle of the space, she was able to make out his semi-naked body, twisted into foetal position, hands bound together, and blood all over the tarmac.

"Shane?"

Shane rolled over on his back momentarily, screamed in pain and back over on his side again. His eyebrow was split, streaming blood. She could see dark ribbons covering his back like a horror film.

"Ah no, Lisa. No. Go away, Ma, go away ... " Her own voice shocked her in its calm.

"Shane love, don't worry, I'm here now, it's okay." She didn't know what to do. Jesus, what was she supposed to do? How could she stop this pain? Part of her wanted to scream too, or just run. Blood pumped from what appeared to be a stab wound on his chest, and she had to press her fingers over it to stem the bleeding. He was writhing in agony, clutching her arm so hard it would be bruised. All she could do was pull his head against her with one hand, and hold his leaking chest with the other.

After a few minutes, like some kind of miracle, the promised ambulance arrived, and they got Shane onto a stretcher. All the way to the hospital, she couldn't understand why he was still in such pain.

"Can't you give him more painkillers?" she begged the paramedic, a young woman with a midlands accent. The girl shook her head.

"Not allowed. They're always like that, you see."

"Like what?"

"Junkies. Pain medicine doesn't have the same effect on them."

"Well, give him more, then, it's not having any fucking effect at all!!"

The girl took a small penlight and shone it with difficulty into Shane's eyes, her latex gloves slippery with blood. She turned back to Lisa recalcitrant.

"You'll have to talk to them in the emergency room."

The girl asked Lisa to sit back and remain calm until they got to the hospital. She did what she was told now, fixing her gaze on Shane's distorted face — the eyes buried in a burgeoning swelling, the jaw somehow wrong, the hands grotesque.

The hospital orderlies looked at her in astonishment as they slid out the gurney. Not your usual bird to come in with a case like this. Inside, it only got worse. She'd heard about this place, generally considered a disgrace to the city, the last of the big old hospitals on the north side, and the only emergency room in the city centre. You could smell the dirt and the decay under the disinfectant, and everything was peeling and grubby and grey, not white, like hospitals should be. An emaciated girl was sitting in a wheelchair, facing the wall of the emergency ward, having difficulty breathing. Nobody appeared to be tending to her.

They pulled Shane onto a bed, and began what looked like a surgical procedure. What, she asked.

"Punctured lung."

They began to do something to Shane that made him scream even louder.

"Give my son another shot!" she roared.

The Indian doctor asked her rather condescendingly to stand back, and that was when she started screaming herself, about giving him another shot, about how the pain medicine wouldn't have the same effect, about how he was only a child, and they began to push her out. She continued screaming, and eventually found herself back outside in the corridor, where she sat down on the smelly tiles beside the girl in the wheelchair and started to cry three year's worth of tears.

Foothills was the best programme in Dublin, they told her. She signed the forms. For the first while, no visits were allowed. Lisa took up smoking again. She got herself to sleep at night usually after a couple of vodkas, and woke up again around 5.30am, with a neck-ache, to worry some more. Then she'd worry all day: in the kitchen, in the car, when she answered the phone, when the phone didn't ring. She spent half her time reading stupid, semi-literate advice books, and the rest talking to doctors and counsellors, only to be more confused than ever.

One appointment was with a disturbingly superior psychiatrist, who spoke to her as if she were a five year-old. Apart from the obvious, Shane was apparently manifesting paranoid schizophrenic tendencies.

"What does "tendencies" mean, exactly, doctor?"

"Well, it's hard to say, Mrs Nolan," answered Dr Snott. "In his current state, you see ... eh ... " he looked at his watch. "It's generally accepted that certain addicts, or indeed alcoholics, are in actuality psychotics administering a form of self-medication. They are often very smart individuals. Your son is a very smart boy."

"*Gifted*," she whispered.

"Pardon?"

"Is his brain destroyed, is what I'm asking you."

"I think we could probably use the term 'obscured', for the moment, Mrs Nolan, until we see what happens after this programme. "

The following Tuesday morning, Lisa awakes with the realisation that today is the first day she is allowed visit Foothills. She does precisely nothing for a couple of hours, listening to the radio. More mass graves found in the Balkans, and The Chieftains in the Carnegie Hall. Around four o'clock, she finds herself nosing up the sweeping drive of the old big-house grounds, metamorphosing for a brief eternity into a bleeding-heart, platform-shod, denim-swathed girl, so inexplicably nervous at the sight of this strange, imposing building coming into focus.

Around the side, where she's been told she will find Shane, she can't believe it that fate actually catches her knocking on a cellar door. She takes a deep breath and purses her lips as a blank faced teenager with dreadful make up opens it, and walks away again into the dimness. Inside, the cracked white tiles of the cellar passage way put a shiver down her spine. Clean, but echoing the horror of twenty years ago. Whatever happened to twenty years, she wonders.

There are bars on the windows. Shadow figures are bobbing in and out of her vision, faces absent or creased with fear. They are very young. She is even younger. She fiddles with the ties of her checked-cheesecloth blouse, bought in the depths of the old Dandelion Green. No, she reminds herself, she is wearing a 100% natural plain-dyed cotton Gap dress - she is not seventeen, Shane is. She forgot. *"On n'est pas serieux quand on a dix-sept ans."*

She wishes Shane's condition were not serious. She wishes he could be sitting on the terrace of some sultry evening café in Paris, ordering beers and lemonade under the linden trees. But that was one of Rimbaud's more innocent poems by far. At this point, "Un Saison dans l'Enfer" would be more appropriate.

The smell is country convent, clean, and with shades on the bulbs. At least that. She wonders what you say to a kid who has almost been beaten to death. Whose eyes have lost their light to be replaced by the sterile glare of emergency rooms and rehab clinics, of helpless mothers and savage criminals. An old memory flashes like a beacon out of her brain's darkness, catches in her throat and creeps liquid into her eyes.

Lisa remembers Bhutan, where she was supposed to travel once, and wonders whether Shane might like to go to a refuge where the humans are so kind, the animals don't fear them. That was something she'd always hoped was true. He might even go for that, she was sure. Because underneath all the lies and the horror, she remembers every moment of his growing, she remembers his smile without defences; she knows that his innate kindness is merely obscured — not destroyed. She has to remember this in order to continue walking into the dining area. The walls are not green, and the chest-high white tiles have no rivulets of damp. She cannot be a coward this time.

He is sitting in the gloomy kitchen corner, silhouetted against the barred window, a trembling cup of instant decaf in his hands, still bandaged.

"Hi, Lisa," he says, barely looking up. "How's it going?"

THE STORY OF A DROWNING

The shock of ice-cold water
stopped his heart.

He jumped in without
a second's thought

when the baby fell
overboard.

It was a glorious day.
The baby floated

oblivious, saved
by a passing boat.

His father's high colour
drained forever —

we could see his face
at the bottom of the lake.

TAKING TEA TO THE MEADOW

For Bríd

Yes, obsession and childhood
memory, a vocabulary both simple
and elusive like the sweetness
of your meadow or the island
of my own salt dream.

SHEILA PHELAN

CUERNAVACA

His step-mother looked me
up and down and said something
he translated as *You are naïve*.

We left the dusty village
and drove to a volcano
called Popocatapetl.

It was a steep climb.
We stopped for crêpes
made by a girl hunkered
by her stove at 2,000 feet.

A mist came down like
something out of Tolkien.
We sheltered in a cabin
and argued as travelers do.

I asked him to leave me
in a hotel in Cuernavaca.
I visited courtyard gardens
and a chapel luminous
in yellow ochre colours.

That evening at the hotel
a waiter watched me swim.
He stood in the shadows
holding a tray.

I plunged, head down,
and when I dared
breathe again he was gone.

Sheila Phelan

VISITING HOUR

When I go to the hospital
my grandmother asks where
I've been and how did I find her.

When I leave she asks if
I have the key.

On sunny days we'd drive
to Malahide Castle.
She'd wait while I parked the car,
white head nodding, remembering
the names of flowers.

"Don't go" she whispers,
her gaunt head barely
lifting off the pillow.

PETROL STATION, HAMBURG

He fills the tank of this huge car,
then slides back in to the driver's seat.

A girl passes in front of the windscreen.
She is younger than she looks,
wearing platform shoes and makeup.

Ein kind he says and I know
he has appraised her, same as me.
I am ashamed for us both.

SHEILA PHELAN

COWBOY POETRY
FROM MY BUSH

ADRIENNE ANIFANT

The cowboy era began during the Gold Rush, around 1849, and lasted only until 1887. Early on, cowboys were more like cowhands for the trail drives across country, who later developed into gunfighters portrayed as protectorates of law and order in the west. Working for only room, board, and tobacco, jobs were seasonal, with roundups taking place in April and the trail drive lasting from May to mid-August. Despite the media's most popular image of a cowboy, forty percent of professional cowboys were black, Mexican, Native American or women.

Henry Kissinger said, "I've always acted alone. Americans admire that immensely. Americans like the cowboy who leads the wagon train by riding ahead alone." Kissinger couldn't have been more accurate. The cowboy represents a crucial figure in American mythology. The lone cowboy's ideals and his story have become the American story; a means through which politicians rationalize their actions, primarily violence. Teddy Roosevelt, Harry Truman, LBJ, George Bush senior and junior, all adopted various aspects of the cultural cowboy in order to manipulate, construct and sell their image.

Vietnam was referred to as "Indian Country." George W. uses cowboy rhetoric, or as Texans still call it, "cowboy poetry" to justify his actions since the World Trade Center fell. Defined by cowboy poet Terry Ike Clanton, cowboy poetry is "everything from stories, poems, tall tales, flat out lies to just plain brag." Bush's inarticulacy is a trademark of the cowboy; the quiet man full of action not words. Osama bin Laden was *Wanted: Dead or Alive*. Now, Saddam Hussein is an *outlaw* and Bush's only objective is "the security of the American people", who according to the right wing *Newsweek* must "go it alone." Using the media, Bush's objective is to portray himself as a common man who works in the field and wears blue jeans, boots and a cowboy hat. George W. takes journalists for a tour "round the 'ol ranch," while dodging their relentless questions concerning his domestic and foreign policy. This simple cowboy who drops "citizens" for "folks" and who axes his verbs with an apostrophe during the State of the Union Address, has acquired the most executive power in the history of the US presidency and has had the highest approval rating during mid-term elections since Franklin D. Roosevelt.

How has this rootin' tootin' wrangler managed to wield so much power and be an idiot? The danger partly lies within the indubitable authority of the lone cowboy image: quick with the gun and slow in the brain, he still defeats evil, or redskins, from terrorizing the townsfolk. Princeton western expert Lee Clark Mitchell wrote, "So self-contained is the later western hero that he seems to exist beyond the everyday commonplaces of talk and explanation, of persuasion, argument, indeed beyond conversation altogether." The image of a fearless gunfighter is a definitive signifier or code of American national pride. A nation's myth used to explain and condone unsolicited violence from an unwarranted arbiter. No matter how he rides us, cowboy ethics always lead to death.

TO THE GLORIOUS DEAD

For their King and their country
and the promise of glory
they went to war.

Bleeding to death
still holding their intestines
with their bare hands,
coughing up their lungs
blinded by the gas
drowning in the mud of Flanders
with their arms stretching out,
shot
they fell to the ground.

Some survived.
Some came back.
Twitching, slobbering or in total silence.

Dr Rivers writes *shell-shock*
on another typed form
watched by staring eyes burdened with
memories too much to bear.

The cenotaph,
now a traffic island,
says "To the Glorious Dead".
But what is glorious about dying?

They promised they would never forget you.
But who is going to make them keep their promise?

The cenotaph says
To the Glorious Dead.

ROSHANARA VOETZSCH

TARPAULIN

Helena Mulkerns

I am blue plastic, a simple thing. Mass produced, distributed in panic, witness to horror, immune to it. I have no weight, no voice, no sight. I am received into the shaking arms of orphaned children, skeletal widows, and with me comes a kind of hope beyond the comprehension of those who finance my manufacture. I have no bones, no arms, no brain, but I am the world's unlikely protector in the places it prefers to forget.

I am a stretcher for a bleeding mine victim. I am shoes, twisted with twine onto a leper's stumps, rainy season. I am the bed on which babies are born, I am the shroud in which massacre victims are covered.

I have been traded for food, bought for sexual favours; I have been a church, a hospital, a school. I have travelled to the world's worst places, to squalid camps too long extant, and never-ending

war zones. I have no heart, no hands, but sometimes I give more than those who do.

My shelter comforts the hopeless, I collect rainwater to alleviate thirst. I envelop bags of grain to keep them dry, I am secured by rough metal-lined perforations, over boxes of medicine on trucks climbing mountain passes to plague-filled outposts. I am a roof, a wall, a house: make me a frame, and I will make you a dwelling for a dozen belly-swelled children. Or a dying room for a moribund mother with AIDS, ignored by government and family. If you see me heaved up against a dusty building, I am the refuge of a scuffle of street urchins, running ragged in the squalor of so-called cities.

From slits in me, the desert eyes of unveiled women peep nervously at their world, watching out for the big white water truck, the white jeep, the white tank, hoping it will be a white tank. Since here, a sad perversion of God's colours makes green the hue of warring military.

In bombed-out villages I provide so many roofs that from overhead choppers I look like one big ruins-and-blue patchwork quilt. What a sorry bed to lie on.

I am a simple thing. I have no love, I have no politics, I am all-seeing of man's brutal follies, although I have no eyes. I ask no recompense, I make no comment, I do so much. I am blue plastic with white letters and a well-meaning symbol that sullies fast with desert dust and mountain muck, until the letters have faded into a shade somewhere between nightmare and desperation. But my blueness stays — all around the world, desert, mountain, riverbank, plain. A humble, dirty, plastic blue, ubiquitous, necessary. Sometimes I am the most that can be done, under the circumstances.

AH SWEET DANCER!

Susan Lanigan

Cliona's mother goes to her daughter's bedroom window and looks out at the back garden. The grass has turned pale with frost and the year-old beech hedge that divides the garden from their couple of acres is bare and brittle. Cliona's father has planted them all close together; that is the way it is done to make sure enough of them can fight their way up through the years to become real trees, mature, unafraid.

There is nothing for miles beyond except pasture; the next house along on the road is a couple of hundred yards down. There is privacy enough for Cliona's mother to stand by the window unwatched. For so many years, she watched out the front window, waiting anxiously. There is no anxiety now. The madness in her has abated.

The bedspread has a nondescript pattern of small fleurs-de-lis on a beige-pink background. A smell of carpet cleaner and dust rises as Cliona's mother walks slowly away from the window in her tan mid-heel shoes. She does not wish to wake her husband again. They have been through enough.

She passes the desk that serves as both a place of study and a vanity stand. An edition of *The Collected Poems of W.B. Yeats* lies open under the mirror. Cliona's English project was supposed to be a reading of "Sailing to Byzantium", the one they all did at school. But the pages would not stay where they were, the breeze flipped them forward to the poem "Sweet Dancer". Cliona liked that one.

> *The girl goes dancing there*
> *On the leaf-sown, new-mown, smooth*
> *Grass plot of the garden;*

Cliona's mother hears a stirring next door. She has learned her husband's ways well over the twenty years of their marriage. As she listens to his turning, she freezes herself in the shadow of the doorway.

A soft gasp from the bedroom, and she knows this time she is in the clear. The gasp quickly deepens into a snore, and she tiptoes out of the room into the big bedroom they have shared without rancour for all this time. As she stands over the bed, unbuttoning her fawn cardigan and leaving her beads on the bedroom table in the patchy February dawn, she recalls, not for the first time, the poem's refrain: "Ah dancer! Ah sweet dancer!"

It was going to be Cliona's first proper night out. And not before bloody time, either. Every single one of her friends was allowed to go out, some of them even went off with the boys. Cliona was a late bloomer. She had once felt the wire in a girl's bra at hockey practice; it had been an accident of course, somebody had tackled somebody else and Cliona's hand on the hockey stick ended up hitting her opponent's breast. There was the oofy feeling of hitting soft tissue and then the scrape of the wire under the Aertex blouse. "Lezzer" the other girl had shrieked, her mouth twisting into a venomous loop. Cliona had not known what she meant.

The problem with Cliona, Nuala said, was that she was just too naïve. Nuala was Cliona's best friend. She was good at helpful suggestions like getting a deodorant to make sure you didn't smell in class, or keeping quiet if you were (like Cliona) the kind to trip out with impulsive tactless comments in a bid to impress the élite. In Burtonhall Convent of Mercy Secondary School for Girls, this consisted of Michelle Murray and her set. Nuala got Michelle, a knife-eyed minx if ever there was one, off Cliona's back. In return, Cliona would let Nuala copy her homework. Especially maths, which Nuala detested.

Nuala had kissed a few boys, one with tongues and all. "He was like a *washing machine*," she whispered, "just round and round and round."

"Ugh." Cliona agreed, though she had never been kissed herself.

"I met him at Katey's the other night and we went off around the side and he just *mauled* me, I mean *everywhere*. His hands ... yeuch!"

Cliona wondered what it would be like if the boy with the roaming hands were to feel *her* body that way. The thought of it tightened her insides; she felt a flush rise from her freckled, hidden cleavage up through her neck to her cheeks. Weird things had been happening since her periods had started. Her mother had been useless. "It's a woman's sacrifice, a woman's sacrifice," she had said, her eyes darting around from side to side. Cliona had not asked her again after that, consulting Nuala and the library instead.

Cliona's mother had what her father and neighbours called The Problem. The Problem meant that she was liable to wander around in blank-eyed trances, or try to run away in the middle of the night. A few years ago they'd put her up in St Brigid's for a while. She had emerged smiling, but dazed. Then the shocks had worn off and The Problem had made a re-appearance. It was really bloody embarrassing sometimes, Cliona thought, but never more so than the times when she was going out the gate and her mother would run after her screaming, "Don't take her away from me! Don't let them take her away! Don't take her!" It was bad enough her pulling that stunt, but it got to the point where she stayed in the front room, looking through the window to spot when Cliona might go out past the gate.

"She never does it when it's you," Cliona grumbled to her father.

He sighed. "She had a hard time when you were a baby. You almost didn't survive, pet. Perhaps her mind keeps harping on to that. They've got better drugs for her now, though, something called Largactil. That might do the trick."

Having a nutcase for a mother made life hard. Cliona had not yet joined the party, but she wanted to; she really, really wanted to. But her father rarely stood up to her mother. He was as afraid of those wandering, restless eyes as she was.

Eventually, her father promised to help. They could not tell her mother honestly, she was strange about things like this. Her hands would turn into claws scrambling at the sky, her eyes would have that terrifying wild look that meant The Problem was going to start. The times when she would wander around the road in her nightdress or stay in her bed for weeks and weeks.

"We won't tell your mother," Cliona's father said.

Katey's was a huge nightclub on the border of three counties. It reared up out of the surrounding farmland like a cathedral spire in the desert. On Friday and Saturday nights, the quiet fields, bathed in their usual moist darkness, would be covered by headlight after headlight as the taxis came in. And not only taxis; some smart fellows turned up in their own Toyota Corollas and Nissan Almeras, ready to wreak havoc on the drunks who were foolish enough to try to walk back the ten miles into town.

Cliona and Nuala stepped out of the car, shivering, their clothes inadequate for the Irish winter. Nuala was wearing a spangly, off-the-shoulder top that offered tantalising hole-shaped views into her cleavage. Her cheeks had been rouged lightly and touched up with glitter. She wore the tightest pair of ski-pants that Cliona had ever seen ("Thongs. An absolute life-saver") but her teeth rattled and she shivered convulsively, even after she had put on the black angora cardigan that looked so neatly tailored in the warm sanctuary of Cliona's bedroom.

The queue to get in moved relentlessly slowly, the big bouncer at the top smacking his lips and waiting to check their ID.

"Just lie," Nuala whispered. "Tell him you lost it and you were born in 1980. *Nine*-teen *Eigh*-ty. That'll make you nineteen and you'll get in no problem."

Verified by the bouncer, their handbags and coats duly ticketed, the girls went up the stairs and into the club. As they passed the huge red baize double doors, a dark wallop of sound spilled out and engulfed them. The place was chock full of people: people hanging off the railings around the bar, people grinding fag butts into the spats of blue carpet around the dance floor with their boot-heels, people whose T-shirts and fringes clung to them wetly as they charged in and out of the Ladies and Gents. The air was heavy with cigarette smoke, dry ice, and the combined sweat of numberless dancers. The DJ was playing "I Just Can't Get Enough" by Depeche Mode. On each chorus, after the "I just can't get enough" line, he made the people on the dance floor raise their fist and yell "Sex!" He chimed in on the whole chorus, going "Sex! Sex! Sex! Sex! Sex!" over the microphone.

"*He* probably isn't getting enough," Nuala said.

After that, he let out even more dry ice. Somebody farted in the middle of the nitrogen fog and it stayed, fixed balefully in the air. Cliona secured herself a little space among the jerking elbows, wobbly breasts and moshers flattening the feet of anyone who got in their way, and started to dance.

Nuala went to the bar and got them both Wee Beasties. "It's like Red Bull only with vodka in it and some sweet stuff like cranberry juice, or something …"

Cliona sipped it, gingerly at first, then in bigger gulps. This stuff was interesting. Nice and sweet, it coated your throat and it took a couple of swallows before you felt that odd, agreeable sort of feeling … Cliona danced again, faster and faster. They were playing Fatboy Slim and everyone was hopping. She couldn't see Nuala in the crowd but it didn't matter.

"*Right here! Right now! Right here! Right now!*"

The lads in their circles didn't bother her now. The narrow-eyed girls with pint in one hand, fag in the other, couldn't touch her. Even if Michelle Murray sidled up to her and whispered into her left ear "Your period's showing through your jeans and everyone can see" she wouldn't care. She just danced.

Nuala came back and poked her in the ribs. Some of the boys they knew had arrived, Tim from the class above them (Nuala's washing machine kisser) and two of his friends, Keelin and Joe.

They ignored her at first. Tim spent the whole time talking to Nuala and his sidekicks just talked about football. Keelin even wore his favourite Glasgow Celtic T-shirt. He was a drink of water of a boy; his chin pulled his whole face downwards in the expression of the perpetually unfulfilled. His lips folded over on themselves and he constantly chewed gum. Cliona could see it in his mouth every time he opened it to shout out an opinion.

Joe, the other one, seemed nicer. He motioned "Another drink?" at her. She nodded and he pointed to the empty Wee Beastie bottle in her hand and raised his eyebrows in a question. She nodded again. He disappeared into the mêlée of people waiting at the bar. While Cliona waited, she watched the dancers and felt the noise of the place fade far away. She swayed slightly and shook herself to recover balance. The heat and the noise made her feel displaced and remote.

Joe came back. "They didn't have Wee Beastie," he shouted, "so I got you a Bacardi Breezer instead." Cliona nodded and fastened her mouth around the neck of the bottle. The drink tasted sickly sweet and she felt another weird twinge go through her. Again she nearly lost her balance and Joe steadied her with a gentle touch on her arm. She smiled at him gratefully. He wasn't too bad, Joe. Had a bit of a pot belly under his yellow Nike T-shirt, it was true, but it wasn't too big. His body was wide and heavy. Not like Keelin's, which tapered down like a telephone pole. Joe's eyes and lips were stretched as if someone had played the "I'm a Chinese" game with them and pulled them towards the sides of his head. They crinkled attractively when he smiled.

The music slowed *subito*. The DJ summoned "all*lll* the lov*errrrsss*" by putting on "Angels" by Robbie Williams — and on cue, the fast movers disappeared to be replaced by couple after couple, gyrating helplessly against each other, mashing faces and bottoms with mouths and hands, grabbing on to each other as if they had just fallen off the *Titanic* and all the lifeboats were taken.

Nuala and Tim were getting close at this point, he brushing her arm as he lifted his drink, she touching his shoulder before shrieking with laughter at something she thought funny. Keelin and Joe vanished, and, as Tim and Nuala made their inevitable way to the dance floor, Cliona realised she was alone in Katey's on a Saturday night in the middle of a slow dance.

"I shouldn't worry," she told herself, "it's just one night, it doesn't mean there's anything wrong with me, they're always trying things on anyway."

But the couples dancing did not let up, rubbing and circling groin-to-groin, kissing each other with deep greed, feeling bottoms and breasts, even diving their hands between each other's legs. She was right — it was a cattle mart. She took another sip of the Bacardi Breezer and looked out at them again. That weird heat was returning to bother her; she could feel herself blush from head to toe. Without thinking, she put her hand on her right breast and gently caressed it round and round with her fingertips; was this what it would be like to be felt up by a boy? Then she caught sight of Joe coming back from the bar and dropped her hand quickly, feeling a second flush of embarrassment. What on earth did she think she was doing?

The music dampened down for a moment.

"You on your own?" Joe asked.

Cliona nodded.

Joe cleared his throat. "Want to come and dance?"
Cliona felt the panic rise like a knot in her chest. She stood there dumbly, not being able to say no, not being able to say yes.

"It's OK," Joe said hurriedly, "I wasn't going to do anything … well, off base, you know? It was just that Keelin's disappeared and you seemed a bit lost on your own there and — "
Cliona nodded Yes.

"So … ?" Joe still looked confused.

"Yes. Yes, I'd love a dance."

Joe grinned at her. "Let's give it a lash, so."

Taking her by the arm, he led her out onto the floor and found them a space amid the mass of heaving bodies. Robbie petered out and was followed by Bryan Adams. Joe placed a respectfully rigid hand on the small of Cliona's back and took her hand with his. They started to move. Right next to them a girl in white hotpants and a matching camisole was kneading her partner's buttocks with increasing speed and licking his face like an ardent dog at the same time. Joe leaned over towards Cliona.

"Ugh. It'd put you off your dinner, wouldn't it?"

Cliona lifted her head to reply. "She probably never *had* her dinner, that's why she looks so hungry now."

Dancing with Joe was nice, different — but for some reason, perhaps out of shyness or lack of inclination, he did not relax his rigidity, he didn't slide his hands downwards or move closer to her. Despite feeling much relieved that he *hadn't* done these things, Cliona also couldn't help feeling faintly disappointed as they moved around, Joe leading expertly. Of course, she hardly knew him, but there were girls a lot uglier than her out there shifting boys, so why should she be excluded? She was just beginning to wonder if it would be totally bad manners for *her* to kiss *him* when they were interrupted by a sharp jolt. Keelin joined them, armed to the hilt with drinks.

"Good on ya, Joe-boy, no flies on you at all," he sneered. Joe went red again and said nothing. The moment had been spoiled.

"A'right, Keelin." He dropped his hold on her as if she were hot metal.

"Not interruptin' anythin', am I?" Keelin was all insincere solicitude.

"No — no, not at all" said Joe. "You got drinks for us there?"

"Sure — got them for everyone. I even got you a Wee Beastie." He winked at Cliona.

"They told me they didn't have any."

"Well, Joe, you obviously hit the wrong barman."

Cliona had to admit to herself that the Wee Beastie tasted marginally better than the Barcardi Breezer, but that was the only consolation. She couldn't believe Joe was so two-faced. Typical stupid Cliona, thinking he might have liked *her*, rather than just being in it for the laugh. She took the drink from Keelin and walked off.

"Lover's tiff?" she could hear him yell after her. "At least have the manners to thank me for the drink, you fat cow."

Cliona blinked back the tears pricking the corners of her eyes. She wasn't going to cry. She was *not* going to cry. She melted into the crowd and became one with the surge of people shoving their way from the dance floor to the toilets. Once she saw the Ladies sign, she bolted through the door in relief, leaving her Wee Beastie bottle for someone else to pick up.

Her hopes of refuge were short-lived. Michelle Murray stood by the mirror, delicately flicking her mascara brush against her eyelashes, opening her eyes wide to get the aim right. When she saw Cliona, she put down the brush, slid it back into her compact and turned around with a full-on catlike smile.

"Well *hello* Cliona Rattigan. I'm surprised to see *you* here."

"Oh hello, Michelle." Despair suddenly stung her into boldness. "I must say I'm not surprised to see *you* here."

The smile vanished and the eyes began to pulse with a green on-and-off glint, the one that invariably signified "trouble ahead".

"Do you mind telling me," Michelle said icily, "what that's supposed to mean?"

Cliona said nothing.

"Cliona?"

Cliona reddened and faced the toilet door that was still showing Engaged. Please finish, please finish, she prayed to herself.

"I'm *waiting*."

Thank Christ, the toilet flushed and the door swung open. One of Michelle's cronies fell out, grey-faced. Michelle's attention was diverted and Cliona fell onto the toilet seat, exhausted. Outside she could hear Michelle's friend's moans, interspersed with the odd annoyed exclamation from Michelle. Then, as the flow of Wee Beasties coursed its way out of her body, Cliona heard an unmistakeable noise.

"UGH!" Michelle's voice was high-pitched with anger. "My *shoes*. My new shoes. You're *disgusting*! *Disgusting*. Get away —

get away from me! Ugh! Ugh! For God's sake." A few more moans, a door banging, and then there was silence.

Cliona left the bathroom without washing her hands. "You're no daughter of mine" her mother would say, but she always said that. Anyway, the sink was full of puke. There was no way she was washing in that.

She could see no sign of Nuala in the crowd but they were playing "Come on Eileen" and she felt the urge to dance again. To hell with Joe, Keelin, the lot of them. She found herself moving to the vibration of the beat coming up from the floor. She closed her eyes and moved faster, fixing her head up to the white spotlight so that she saw crazy bright shapes behind her eyelids.

Then, like Cinderella, she remembered the time.

Oh my God. Five to twelve, and she was still stuck in here.

Her mother would go mad. She'd go on and on with the usual rubbish and then wind up saying "I never had you". That was the point when Cliona's father would come and put a hand on her mother's shoulder, say her name and lead her up to bed to give her the "dose".

She couldn't handle the guilt. Not this time.

She got off the dance floor and looked frantically for Nuala. She found her, finally, around the corner from the Gents, interlocked with Tim.

"Nuala! Nuala!"

"Oh for God's sake." Nuala was irritable at being interrupted. "What is it?"

"I have to go home."

"Ah Cliona, do you have act like you're in nappies? It's hardly twelve. Just chill out and have the consideration to *wait* a while, will you?"

"But my mother said — "

"Your mother!" Nuala said, with peculiar venom. "Your flippin' mother is touched in the head, Cliona. Everyone knows that. Tell *your mother* to get a life and take whatever pills she needs to calm down and leave *me* alone."

Cliona stared at her.

Nuala stared back. "Well, *go*, then," she said, and resumed kissing Tim.

Cliona staggered back as if she had been dealt a blow. Anger surged towards her mother. Embarrassing her all the time, crying and acting like that. Making sure she had no friends and no life.

I hate her, Cliona thought. And she realised it was true. Had always been true.

She walked quietly past the drunks who were drooling onto tables, unaware of her presence, and on to the cloakroom attendant who took her ticket and returned all the things, including Nuala's.

"No, just these." Cliona said. "I don't care what happens to the other things."

"Pardon?"

"Just leave them!" she snapped.

He shrugged his shoulders. "OK, you're the boss."

She walked out the front entrance, unaware that an argument was going on about her inside. Joe, Nuala, Tim and Keelin were gathered around the bar.

"I thought she was with you."

"You never let her go home on her own, Nuala?" Joe was shocked.

"Well she wanted to leave so early. She just does whatever her mother says."

"You didn't do that on my account, did you, Nuala?"

"For God's sake, Tim, of course I didn't," Nuala lied tersely.

"We'd better go find her — or something — " Joe made to move, but no one else showed a sign of joining in.

"Well , er … are we …"

"Ah," Tim mused, "she'll probably be OK."

Joe sighed and sat back down again.

"Yeah." Keelin said. "No point going out there, we won't be able get back in." He smiled. "Another drink?"

"I'll have a Wee Beastie, please," Nuala said.

December hit Cliona the minute she went outside. Rain had begun to fall, a gentle drizzle by itself, a killer alongside the sharp-edged wind. Too late, Cliona remembered Nuala had her cardigan, the one her mother gave her. Oh if only she had the black monstrosity now! It looked awful but at least it would have kept her warm. The heartbeat of the music inside contrasted with the desolate quiet all around. Here, there was only the wind sighing through the hawthorn hedges, the rain beating softly down.

She saw no sign of a taxi. She tried the payphone in the entrance, but it had no dial tone. She shivered again. There were two alternatives: wait it or walk it. Cliona calculated the distance: Burtonhall was a mile out in the direction of Katey's, and Katey's was about another mile out … it was doable. Anything was better than waiting in this cold, standing outside the warm, throbbing building that did not want her.

Feeling the foundation on her skin beginning to melt with the rain, she thought about the night, touching a boy for the first time, Michelle's tantrum at her friend puking over her shoes. Nuala's anger. Then the dance, dance, dance. Cliona realised that although she didn't have much of a knack with boys, and she didn't like smoke, and alcohol made her lose her balance and giggle too much, she loved to dance. And so she started, on the road back from Katey's nightclub on the border of three counties, to dance again, leaping along the bare, silent road, letting the rain course through her hair, singing wildly to herself. Remembering the Yeats poem she had read in the collection, about the madwoman who had fallen in love with Yeats and been locked up in a mental hospital, the same way her mother had been. But she had been a crazy, beautiful dancer and Yeats had loved her. She was in the dance, she was happy, in spite of it all, so happy.

If strange men come from the house
To lead her away, do not say
That she is happy being crazy;
Lead them gently astray;
Let her finish her dance,
Let her finish her dance.
Ah, dancer, ah, sweet dancer!

And that was where a drunk driver, under the condition of Garda anonymity, reported the last known sight of Cliona Rattigan. After that ... only the fields swollen with rain and their scrawny hedgerows could bear witness. It was as if they had noiselessly swallowed her up; the only sounds that year (and all the years after) anyone heard were pidgeon-coos, rustling leaves, and the sound of Garda vans on their fruitless trawl up and down the clean verges of the road, seeking some clue to where she had gone. She, like the six others who disappeared before her, were never seen again.

One walking into Newbridge to get money out of the bank machine. One hitching a lift out of Moone to Castledermot after she had missed the bus. One hiking in the Wicklow mountains, lost between the Sally Gap and the round tower. God only knew what happened to the rest.

As time passes, the questioning dies down. Nobody except the families, with no body to bury, still concern themselves. While they want to hope, the younger sister eventually moves into the bedroom, the clothes and boxes are put away in storage. If the lost girls were to return, it would be as frightening as if they had come back from the dead.

Cliona Rattigan's name is public property now. When the case was at its height, there were journalists all over the town. Nuala stopped going to Katey's. Her mother put her foot down. Nuala didn't really go out much more after that anyway. Rumour had it that later on she got pregnant and dropped out of school. Pleurisy, the headmistress called it. Pregnancy, more like, the women snorted, and hadn't she been pally with that wan who ...

Then they stopped speaking and crossed themselves.

Her mother is not troubled by any speculation about what happened to Cliona. There is no thought so ghastly and torturous that it can trouble her now, of how she might have met her end, if indeed she had. Her eyes are no longer restless. They have already seen the worst that she predicted. The madness has gone. Cassandra can only prophesy once before the gods destroy her.

And that is how, four years later, calm and unmedicated, Cliona's mother can look out the window at the back garden without tears springing to her eyes. She, alone among the mothers, was always calm.

Cliona's father planted all the beech trees close together; that is the way it must be done. Some of them will be choked out so the others can survive, grow tall, make a wood. That is the way of nature. Later on, he will call out to her mother, "Carmel, is dinner ready?" and she will sing back, "'Tis indeed Anthony, just give us a minute with the sauce."

ABOUT THE AUTHORS

ADRIENNE ANIFANT is originally from Hyde Park, New York. She graduated from Mount Holyoke College with a degree in Anthropology and English. She has been published in the *Women's Studies Review* and *The Review of Postgraduate Studies*, and is currently pursuing a Masters in Writing at the National University of Ireland, Galway (NUIG).

SANDRA BUNTING has written for various newspapers and magazines in Canada. Her poetry has appeared in *Time Haiku*, London and *Crannóg*, Galway. She is working on her Masters in Writing at NUI Galway, preparing a poetry collection and hopes to finish a novel in the near future.

BENJAMIN COOMBS is a music journalist and broadcaster who has been published in *Hot Press* and *Q*, among other publications. He is a graduate of the University of Kent, and is currently completing a Masters in Writing at NUIG. *Nightswimming* is his first published story.

BARRY FERNS has spent the last six years writing and performing comedy for stage, television and radio in London and at the Edinburgh festival. His work as a stand-up comedian was described as "bold original and fresh" by *The Scotsman*. He is currently writing a radio series and play along the ideas of "poetic terrorism" and a stage show for the Edinburgh festival about death.

GERARD HANBERRY is a poet from Galway who is currently doing the MA in Writing at NUIG. He was shortlisted for the Hennessy Award for poetry and won the Listowel Writer's Week Original Short Story Competition in 2000. A collection of his poetry, entitled *Rough Night* was published in 2002.

SUSAN LANIGAN worked as a programmer with FKM/Hewlett Packard before deciding to concentrate full time on her writing. She won an award from the President of NUIG for her play, *Sister Nobody*, which premiered at the *Muscailt* Festival in Galway. She has been published in *Electric Acorn* and *The Stinging Fly*.

CATRIONA MITCHELL was born in Switzerland and educated in Scotland and Australia. She now divides her time between the two hemispheres in an attempt to craft life into one long summer. She has written for *Index on Censorship*, *Source Magazine*, *Irish Theatre Magazine*, *Sunday Miscellany*, and was ghost-writer on *Seven Principles for Radiant Living* by Jason Chan.

MIKE MC CORMACK's acclaimed fiction collection *Getting It in the Head* won the 1995 Rooney Prize and his first novel, *Crowe's Requiem*, was published by Jonathan Cape. He has just finished his second novel, and is the 2003 Writer In Residence at NUIG.

MARION MOYNIHAN started writing poetry seven years ago when she joined Fia Rua Writers' Group in Killarney. She was short-listed for the Strokestown Prize in 2000 and has been published in *The Sunday Tribune* among other publications. She is currently studying for a Masters in Writing at NUIG, and is on the lookout for a publisher.

HELENA MULKERNS has written for *Hot Press*, *The Irish Times*, *The Sunday Tribune*, *Elle*, *Rolling Stone*, *Cinéaste*, *The Irish Echo* and more; her short stories have been broadly anthologised and she was short-listed for the Hennessy Literary Award and the American Pushcart Prize. She has worked for UN Peacekeeping missions in Guatemala, Ethiopia and Eritrea and is currently completing an MA in English Literature and Publishing at NUIG. (http://siar.net)

SHEILA PHELAN has had poems published in *The Stinging Fly*, *The SundayTribune*, *Samhlaíocht Chiarraí and ROPES*, and was shortlisted for the Hennessy Prize and Fingal Scribe. She has also worked with *Poetry Ireland*. She was awarded an Arts Council Bursary for Literature in 2002. Her first play, *19-23*, a one-act, was performed during the Muscailt Festival at NUI, Galway, 2003.

STEPHEN SHIELDS presently lives in Athenry with his wife, Anne, and daughters, Ciara and Eimear. A dog called Bruce, who wandered in and liked the company, and two cats, complete the household. He has worked as a lawyer, but his career was interrupted by a serious bout of illness. The silver lining to this cloud was that he rediscovered his interest in writing, and has since published both poetry and short stories.

ROSHANARA VOETZSCH (Jules) is a graduate of Goldsmiths College, University of London, and came to Ireland to pursue a Masters in Writing in NUIG. Since returning to London, she has been working in publishing and on several of her own writing projects. She is also seeking a publisher for her first novel, on the French Revolution.

MISJA WEESJES spent the first half of her life in The Netherlands, and has since been living in Galway, where she has been writing, among other things. She is currently in the final stages of her Masters in Writing at NUIG. She is starting to publish some of her work, and is in the process of completing her first novella.

PHOTOGRAPHS

p.12 Honduras, border town plaza at midday
p.14 Deserted promenade, Assab port, Eritrea
p.43 Parisian cats looking superior in Montmartre
p.57 Somewhere in the Red Sea, a dolphin swam beside our boat
p.72 Prehistoric grave mound at Knowth, Ireland
p.82 Sun filigree tree, Kenya
p.87 Evening, Lake Tana, Ethiopia
p.102 Volcano and cloud mirrored in Lake Atitlán, Guatemala
p.108 Camp for Internally Displaced People, Africa

All photographs copyright © of Helena Mulkerns

Siar Press